D0836618

PRAISE FOR
101 WAYS TO TORTURE YOUR HUSBAND

"Deliciously devilish . . . and downright hilarious! Love it!"

—Jill Zarin, *The Real Housewives of New York City*

"When your beloved asks you, 'How could you even THINK of reading such a mean book?' Just say, 'No pain, no gain!'"

—Dalma Heyn, author of *Marriage Shock: The Transformation of Women into Wives* and *Drama Kings: The Men Who Drive Strong Women Crazy*

"A perfect blend of fantasy and laughter. I wish all my patients would read this book!"

—Manhattan therapist Carrie Gelber Rosenfield, PsyD

101 WAYS TO TORTURE YOUR HUSBAND

101 WAYS TO TORTURE YOUR HUSBAND

Maria Garcia-Kalb

Aadamsmedia

Avon, Massachusetts

Copyright © 2010 by Maria Garcia-Kalb
All rights reserved.
This book, or parts thereof, may not be reproduced in any
form without permission from the publisher; exceptions are
made for brief excerpts used in published reviews.

Published by
Adams Media, a division of F+W Media, Inc.
57 Littlefield Street, Avon, MA 02322. U.S.A.
www.adamsmedia.com

ISBN 10: 1-60550-010-0
ISBN 13: 978-1-60550-010-2

Printed in the United States of America.

10 9 8 7 6 5 4 3 2 1

Library of Congress Cataloging-in-Publication Data
is available from the publisher.

This publication is designed to provide accurate and authoritative information with
regard to the subject matter covered. It is sold with the understanding that the publisher is not engaged in rendering legal, accounting, or other professional advice.
If legal advice or other expert assistance is required, the services of a competent
professional person should be sought.
　　　—From a *Declaration of Principles* jointly adopted by a Committee of the
American Bar Association and a Committee of Publishers and Associations

Many of the designations used by manufacturers and sellers to distinguish their
product are claimed as trademarks. Where those designations appear in this book
and Adams Media was aware of a trademark claim, the designations have been
printed with initial capital letters.

Certain sections of this book deal with activities that may be potentially hazardous,
dangerous, or illegal. The authors, Adams Media, and F+W Media, Inc. do not accept
liability for any injury, loss, legal consequence, or incidental or consequential damage incurred by reliance on the information or advice provided in this book.

This book is available at quantity discounts for bulk purchases.
For information, please call 1-800-289-0963.

This book is dedicated to my late grandmother, Maria "Machulina" Lajara, who epitomized the term "power woman," and to my son, Ethan, whom I hope will someday make an excellent husband.

DISCLAIMER: The suggestions discussed here are for ENTERTAINMENT PURPOSES ONLY. That means don't be calling me in the middle of the night asking me for bail money. THIS IS JUST FOR FUN AND AMUSEMENT, AND NOT INTENDED TO SERIOUSLY HURT YOUR SIGNIFICANT OTHER IN ANY WAY.

(I hope my attorneys are happy now. Let's move forward.)

Acknowledgments

Special thanks to everyone who helped make this book a reality, especially my husband, Andrew, for his incredible sense of humor, and our son, Ethan, for putting up with me during this bewildering process. I'm also eternally grateful to my parents, Miguel and Victoria, for their love and support, as well as my dear sister Vicky for helping me dream big.

Great thanks to my agent, Linda Konner, and my editors, Andrea Norville and Wendy Simard, for their wisdom and guidance. My closest and dearest girlfriends (a.k.a. "my coven") deserve special mention: Patty "Gayle" Gonzalez, Margaret, Tina, and Paula—I couldn't have done this without you! Many others were also crucial in this process, including Alan Halpern, Edward Cannata, Tia Nancy, the Kalb family, Dave and Robin Dworkin, Jack Fintz, Mike, Julie, Gnarls, Irene, and my incredibly supportive radio listeners for nurturing my female soul and giving me inspiration beyond words.

Contents

Introduction

Hi, my name is Maria and I enjoy torturing my husband.

Okay, I said it. I can't deny it anymore. No more secrets, no more wishing I was "normal," or feeling guilty about it! My husband is a constant pain in my ass and it feels good to get that out in the open.

Now it's your turn.

Don't worry, you'll do fine.

Clear your throat and say aloud:

"Hi, my name is (your name here) and I enjoy torturing my husband—or at least thinking about it!"

Excellent, welcome aboard! You have now joined a sacred trust of once-happy women who married some silly loaf believing her life would be picture-perfect, only to discover that husbands and marriage aren't always the thrill ride we expected them to be. Yep, sometimes we'd like to forget those lovely wedding vows (promising to love, honor, and cherish) and replace them with something more like, "I promise not to strangle my husband on those days when he makes my blood boil and I can't stand to even look at him!" Men can definitely be delightful creatures (on their good days) but they can also be your worst nightmare—morphing into maniacal meanies who make you wonder, "What happened to that kind, considerate, helpful guy I married? Is he EVER coming back?" Now, I know what you're thinking: "Maria, if your husband is so awful, then why are you still married?"

Great question, and here's your answer: Despite the constant frustration, therapy bills, and occasional fits of rage, I still truly *love* my husband. I just don't *like* him all the time. (And according to my therapist, that's perfectly okay!) In fact, I'd like to save you thousands in therapy right now, because after years of soul-searching, useless bickering, and worrying that my marriage would eventually end in divorce, I have come upon an eye-opening revelation: Most husbands are created equal, so it's better to keep the one you have (and just hope he doesn't snore!).

We've all seen it happen. People get divorced, swear they'll never get married again, and before you know it love (or lust cleverly *disguised* as love) rears its ugly head. So they end up remarrying, continuing the vicious cycle of cohabiting with a total stranger who makes them as crazy as the first person they promised to spend all of eternity with! Eternity ain't easy folks, and marriage can be a bitch sometimes—no matter whom you're married to! The truth is the JOURNEY of marriage is the real magical experience (just make sure to pack lots of extra patience because you'll definitely need it along the way!). So when did I come up with the idea of torturing my husband? Let's just say that when I came to the realization that husbands and wives speak an entirely different language, I knew I was in for some serious marriage frustration. At that point, I figured stealth torture was the only way to go. It's all about getting even—without bloodshed or divorce attorneys. So the next time your husband takes you for granted or simply acts like an ass, just pick up your trusty manual (this book), find a fun way to inflict some pain, and get your revenge on!

I have included the following Risk Indicator Alert Chart to guide you along. Here's the breakdown:

RISK INDICATOR ALERT CHART
5 *Run Like Hell*
4 *Watch Your Back*
3 *He Might Be On to You*
2 *Caution, Girlfriend*
1 *You're in the Clear*

As you read along, each torture exercise will have a corresponding risk indicator so you can decide how far you really want to go. Let the games begin!

Chapter One

MENTAL TORTURE

1 Hide the Remote

Ladies, it's time to hit him where it really hurts! No, not there—in the boob tube! After a long draining day at the office most men can't wait to get home and relax in front of a huge (state-of-the-art flat-screen) TV and watch endless hours of mind-numbing programming, which turns them into drooling couch

RISK INDICATOR: 1
You're In the Clear
He'll never know about your devious deed unless your dog digs up the evidence!

potatoes. Those demonic electronic contraptions have managed to manipulate our men, taking up their spare time when they could be doing useful things like putting out the garbage, mowing the lawn, or treating us to a foot massage. We are now forced to compete for our man's attention with this sinister talking box! So it's time to eliminate the enemy—even if it's just for a day. While I would love to make the television disappear altogether, that would be a bit obvious, so I suggest you take a more subtle approach and play "hide and seek" with the remote! This exercise doesn't require much effort. Just sit back and watch the madness unfold as your guy desperately tries to locate the key to his happiness. Your husband will enter the room looking like a junkie who can't wait for his next fix, and after being unable to quickly locate his object of desire, the search and rescue mission begins. Watch your husband toss the throw pillows haphazardly, hoping to turn up the remote. He'll search under the furniture and start to look very concerned. You'll then hear the inevitable question: "Honey, have you seen the remote?" To which you answer, "Oh, the remote? The last time I saw, it was on the coffee table." (Of course, you've buried the evidence in the backyard with childish delight!) Following the thorough perimeter sweep, your husband's frustration will elevate greatly, sending him into a frantic scramble with bulging beads of sweat forming on his furrowed brow. Before you know it, a grown man is reduced to a desperate, weeping heap of misery—and if you're lucky, he'll throw a tantrum that puts a bratty two-year-old to shame. Get your cameras ready!

PROOF POSITIVE

According to the Nielsen Company, the average American male watches 4 hours and 15 minutes of TV each day. If you do the math, that equals more than 29 hours per week, and over 2 straight months of nonstop TV watching per year. By the time an average man is 65 years old he'll have wasted a grand total of 10 years glued to the tube! Frightening, but true.

2 Fake It and Tell Him You Did

Oh, don't act so shocked. You've done it plenty of times, but this time he'll actually know about it! This is a great exercise for a man who needs a massive ego check because it will force him to get his head out of the clouds (and his arse) and cater to your needs for a

RISK INDICATOR: 2
Caution, Girlfriend
You can risk damaging his performance forever! Beware!

change. Most of us don't need to prepare for this kind of task (since we tend to be fantastic fakers when the opportunity presents itself), but for those in need of a refresher, just think of Meg Ryan's unforgettable scene in When Harry Met Sally. You want to put on the best show possible so he'll really be baffled later on.

Ladies, I must digress here, and say that if you are faking on a regular basis, QUIT IT! You are just not being fair to yourself. If sex with your hubby doesn't regularly end in climax, that's like revving up your car engine for a half hour and then turning off the ignition. All you did was get hot and bothered for no reason! If your man can't get you there, seek professional help. Faking only benefits the man and leads him to falsely believe he's "The Orgasm King" . . . BUT this is why we can use it against them. So get loud, get wild, and then tell him the real truth. He'll be floored.

PROOF POSITIVE

According to the 2007–2008 Durex Global Sex Survey, 48 percent of women admitted to faking orgasm. Durex also revealed that Americans are sex-starved, having relations just 85 times a year (about once every 4.3 days), which is way below the global average of 103 times annually. The Japanese have some serious sexual issues, gettin' busy only 48 times per year. Evidently Nigeria is the most sexually satisfied nation, with 67 percent of respondents giving their sex life a thumbs-up.

3 "Lose" His Dog

Ever wonder why dogs are called "man's best friend"? Some might refer to ancient times when man befriended wild wolves, studied their hunting skills, and became better hunters. But I think dogs are called "man's best friend" because when we get fed up with our men and kick them out of the house, Fido is just about the only warm-blooded creature that'll have him!

RISK INDICATOR: 4
Watch Your Back
Men can definitely be vindictive SOBs when it comes to their canine companions, so be prepared for a possible counterattack when he finds out the joke's on him!

The bottom line is, men and their dogs share a unique bond, and that's a win-win for us. Man's best friend can quickly become a woman's perfect tool for torture given the right circumstances—and a deliciously sinister plan. How far you take this one depends on how much torture you want to inflict. Call your hubby at work and in a panicked voice announce, "Oh my God! The dog ran away when I opened the door, and I can't find him anywhere!" After he flips out you can let him in on your little joke and (hopefully) you can both laugh about it. If you want to push it, have one of your friends dog-sit for the day and let the tension build.

Note: The only issue with this plan is that it does put you in the "dog house" (so to speak) because he will most likely blame you for being careless and "losing" the dog. If you decide to go with the extreme version of this exercise, I recommend telling him you just came home and the dog was gone. Just like that. Gulp! He'll feel anguish and fear all at once thinking someone actually violated his home turf and made off with his pal. Now, I'm a devoted animal lover and it makes me terribly sad to think of a pet being stolen, or running away, but the fact is doggie doo happens, so why not take advantage of it? It's not like the pooch will know what really happened, and your husband will be so overjoyed to have his buddy back he may actually forget to give you crap about it.

4 Convince Him He Has a Mysterious Ailment

Have you been on Webmd? They should just call it "youmayhavecancer.com"!—JERRY SEINFELD

Has this ever happened to you? You're talking to one of your friends and she's describing every awful detail of some strange ailment she's dealing with. You listen patiently, evaluating the situa-

> **RISK INDICATOR: 1**
> *You're in the Clear*
> Just think how incredibly relieved and happy he'll be when he discovers he's perfectly healthy!

tion, hearing about her doctor's advice, and wincing sympathetically when you're told about the horrific treatment plan your friend must now endure. Whether it's a fast-spreading skin rash, hideous gastrointestinal condition, or an unusual mind-altering disorder, you suddenly begin some mental checklist of the symptoms your friend has described. Fever; check. Swollen eyelids; check. Recent travel to Pompeii and the Federated States of Micronesia; check. Panic and despair; check. Yep, you are immediately convinced that you too are now carrying said rare condition, and before you know it dizziness, heart palpitations, and general malaise take over, rendering you completely useless (and in need of intense therapy). As we all know, the mind can be easily influenced, and depending on the individual you can actually convince someone he is truly sick by merely making a small observation about his appearance.

Sample: "Hey Bob . . . are you feeling all right? You don't look so good."

Until that moment Bob was feeling utterly fantastic. Now he's wondering what could possibly be wrong with him. "Do I really look sick?" he wonders. "Could I be coming down with something?" "Hmm . . . I did feel kind of dizzy when I got up this morning." That's all any of us need to reroute our thinking, send the wrong messages to the brain, and make ourselves start to believe that something is seriously wrong, when in reality we couldn't be better! This is precisely why making your man think he's contracted a mysterious illness is so amusing. Since the mind is easily influenced (and his is already bogged down with random sports stats) it should be a pretty easy task. So which mysterious illness should you go with? Well, it's your lucky day, because there's a website solely dedicated to bizarre conditions many of us have never even heard of! Just go to *www.rarediseases.org* and find your favorite.

While you pick one, here are some great lines you can use to get the ball rolling:

"You know, there's this new virus going around. You should really get checked out."

Or point to any scrape or pimple and say, "Honey, you know, that could be MRSA. You know, that rare, life-threatening staph infection?" I realize it sounds mean, but it's just a harmless joke. There's nothing wrong with playing suggestive mind-control games on occasion. However, if your husband becomes bedridden and paralyzed with fear, you know you've gone too far. But watching the panic set in will be fun . . . at least at first.

5 Repeatedly Ask Him If You Are Fat

Let's say you are 5'5" and weigh 120 pounds. You are officially NOT FAT, but because we are women, we are forever battling the mirror, wishing we could lose another five pounds and have stick arms like Angelina Jolie. Men are well aware of women's ridiculous insecurities, and they try to assure us that they love us just the way we are, but somehow that's just not enough and we are constantly driven to ask the dreaded question, "Honey, do I look FAT?" While some of the male persuasion have been foolish enough to actually answer that loaded question, 99.9 percent of men understand this is positively un-answerable,

> **RISK INDICATOR: 3**
> **He Might Be On to You**
> Brace yourself for something you may not want to hear. When it comes to comments about appearance and weight, women are as volatile as dynamite, so it's best to prepare for the worst. He also might say something really mean to teach you a lesson and forgo future fat questions. Hope for the best and make sure your cover isn't blown.

and manage to dance around it when it falls from a woman's lips. However, as a means of torture, this question works like a charm because no matter how your man replies, you'll simply refuse to let him off the hook, and make it a point to take everything he says extremely personally and blame him for causing massive emotional damage.

When I'm in the mood to torture my guy I clean out my closet, which necessitates trying on *every* piece of clothing I own. I appoint my husband "Fashion Coordinator" and ask him to help me get rid of any crappy outfits cluttering my wardrobe. He agrees (since men love to be in charge) and off we go. My naive partner has no idea what's about to hit him. He thinks he's helping, but the truth is he's just been set up in the cruelest way.

I strip down to my undies and start squeezing into the most unflattering duds. My husband has no way out. He can't possibly say anything remotely nice after seeing my fat-rolls jammed into a tight tube top, so he's left with no choice but to say I don't look so hot wearing these heinous getups. Therefore, anything he says can be magically transformed to a fat insult. He'll say, "Honey, I'm not sure that's the best look for you." I'll say, "So you're trying to tell me I look FAT AS A HOUSE, RIGHT?"

And the tension builds. No matter how much he denies it, you just accuse him of calling you a blubber monster and hurting your fragile self-esteem. Continue trying on outfits and he'll become more and more anxious. At this point, he's well aware that the next words he utters could unleash a violent flood of screaming and weeping. Make it your best acting role ever, and you might even end up with a new wardrobe in the end as he tries to suck up to make everything better.

PROOF POSITIVE

From the *Journal of Human Sexuality*: Fat phobia is defined as an excessive fear and dislike of fat in oneself and in others. Fear of fat has caused women in particular to reject their bodies and allow their obesity to take on negative meanings that profoundly affect them in many ways, especially their sexuality. Conversely, according to the Social Issues Research Centre, men generally have a more positive body image than women.

6 Flirt with His Friends

Is your husband a jealous fella? Well, this punishment is so devilishly delightful, it must be reserved for only very rare occasions when your husband has been extremely naughty and deserves some serious punishment. (Like, for example, when you catch him flirting with one of *your* friends!) If you flirt with a random stranger your husband might become uncomfortable, but he'll certainly notice if you put the moves

RISK INDICATOR: 4
Watch Your Back
Flirting is always acceptable; flirting with your man's friends could make for broken hearts and possibly broken noses. Choose your moment and victim wisely, and know when to rein it in!

on one of his buddies! This is an excellent tactic, and it's a surefire way to stir up the little green-eyed monster who lives inside every man (whether he wants to admit it or not!). Let's face it: Even the most secure person has felt the burn of jealousy at some juncture, and we all know it can make us do crazy things (but hopefully not *too* crazy!) Here's a foolproof plan.

Step 1: Decide which of your husband's close friends is a total hottie. (It's a tough job, but somebody's gotta do it!) If your husband happens to be the hottie in his group, consider yourself a lucky gal, and move on to the next best thing—his best friend or the pal your husband always competes with. You see, men are highly competitive by nature, so picking the buddy he finds the most threatening (especially if that guy's single) will really get the job done!

Step 2: Be a gracious hostess: Invite your unknowing accomplice over for a family dinner, and don't forget to wear that lovely low-cut blouse your husband hates, or slip into that skirt with the slit up to there! You could also arrange an adult pool party, which gives you the perfect opportunity to wear a sexy swimsuit, or plan a fun night out where you can zone in on your target.

Step 3: Flirt till you drop! Make sure your husband is in earshot when you approach his hot friend and say something like, "Wow, have you been working out? You look fantastic!" Another good one is, "That's a great shirt, Brad, looks good on you!" (My husband nearly dropped his drink at a holiday get-together when I turned to his closest bud and said, "I had the strangest dream about you the other night!") Another approach is to make some kind of physical contact; for example, smooth an out-of-place hair, fix his tie, or wipe his face after a messy mouthful.

Most important, remember to smile excessively, and toss your hair—sure signs that you are flirting, and guaranteed to make your husband wild with jealousy. Trust me, even if your husband pretends it doesn't bother him, believe me, it *does*, and if he actually gets angry, just think about how great the make-up sex will be!

7 Talk Until His Ears Bleed

A husband looking through the paper came upon a study that said women use 30,000 words per day, while men only use about 15,000 words per day. Excited to prove to his wife that he had been right all along when he accused her of talking too much, he showed her the study results. The wife thought for a while, then finally she said to her husband, "It's because we have to repeat everything we say."

> **RISK INDICATOR: 1**
> *You're in the Clear*
> If he's not used to hearing you flap your gums at this point, he needs to get with the program, or at the very least purchase some ear plugs.

The husband said, "What?"

It's no surprise women can talk till infinity. We *are* the smarter sex, after all, and with that heavy burden comes the gift of gab. But, why is it that men are so unnerved by women running their mouths, and why do men really speak less? Is it by choice (because they'd rather be watching ESPN), or is there a definitive biological reason why men are less loquacious? Here's what the latest research shows: A 2008 report in the journal *Neuropsychologia* links language disparities to the way males and females process information. When completing linguistic abilities tasks, girls showed greater activity in brain areas dealing with language encoding, and it turns out we decipher information abstractly. Boys, on the other hand, showed a lot of activity in regions tied to visual and auditory functions, eventually helping them decipher the presented language during the research. So it all boils down to a clear-cut conclusion:

Men aren't too bright. Keep language simple. Use pictures whenever possible.

You know, after discovering this important piece of information, I kind of feel sorry for men. It's not like they had any control over this; it turns out biology set them up to be quasi hearing and language impaired. Therefore, BITCHING is essentially the best way to torture your man linguistically and send his brain into overload! It's true that talking incessantly does the job, but that coupled with constant complaining makes for a powerful double whammy. Complain about anything and everything. Make stories longer and even more detailed (if that's remotely possible). Tell your husband what people were doing, eating, wearing, while you were having an exchange. Discuss anything that can be discussed, tell him about that wacky dream you had last night, and embellish it to death. Elaborate any story or discussion as much as possible, follow him around if you have to, and maybe, just maybe, his head will implode. (What a fantastic story to share with your girlfriends later—over cocktails, of course!)

8 Sabotage His Car

A car represents to a man what designer shoes represent to a woman: toe-curling ecstasy. I can definitely understand why most men are obsessed with their vehicles. A car is a very defining symbol, and it says more about us than we even know.

RISK INDICATOR: 5
Run Like Hell

Beware: Mess with a man's car and you are definitely cruisin' for a bruisin'!

A car study commissioned by BMW echoes this. The study, called "The Secret Life of Cars and What They Reveal About Us," says vehicles feed into a man's need for ownership and possession, their desire to belong, and their hunger for social acceptance (poor, insecure bastards). When discussing cars, men can speak with great confidence (since women have no clue about the topic) and talk to other men openly about their passion for "all things vehicular." It is one topic that generally engages males into conversation, whether they are the casual car lover or suffering from deep-rooted fixation.

For me, a car is a necessary evil, one of those "have-to-deal-with things," because they are quite useful in getting from point A to point B without having to do something unbearable like walking to a determined destination. Yes, cars are extremely useful and convenient, but obsessing over them is just not my bag, baby. It's another one of those "man things," requiring high levels of testosterone flowing through your veins to fully understand. So if you've ever dealt with a serious car freak, you know they are severely infatuated with their vehicles in every way (cleaning them constantly, buying all kinds of car accessories to keep them in tiptop shape . . . some even *name* their cars!) That's not even the worst of it. Some really nutty guys won't even consider letting anyone else drive their precious vehicles. Therefore a successful car switcheroo will cause your man to come undone, leading to substantial mental anguish.

Here are some naughty things you can do when he's not around:

- Turn up the stereo full blast so when he enters the car he'll jump off his seat.
- Change all his radio presets, and replace them with static-filled AM stations.
- Move all the mirrors, especially the rearview . . . it's a bitch to set perfectly.
- Recline the seats as far as they go, and move them back all the way too.
- Empty out the contents of his glove compartment.
- Switch the wipers to the "on" position.
- Take one of your pets for a ride and let him go wild in the car.
- Enjoy some drive-through food and leave the leftovers to rot underneath his seat.

He'll be cursing the day he let you get ahold of his keys!

9 Become a Co-Dependent Nightmare

I know this can be a tough one for fiercely independent gals, but trust me girlfriend, you can do it—and best of all, you might actually enjoy it! Becoming a co-dependent wife is actually the easiest thing on earth because it requires you to do absolutely NOTHING, ZILCH, ZERO,

RISK INDICATOR: 3
He Might Be On to You
Don't go overboard with the "damsel in distress" routine or he might catch on to your game.

NIL, NADA. You merely ask for your husband's help and guidance to do even the slightest, most miniscule task, letting him believe you are utterly helpless without him. At first he may actually like the "new you" (because men think we can't function without them), and he'll be happy to let you know *exactly* how you should handle that problem you're having with your supervisor at work, or what you should do about that leak in the kitchen, and when is the right time to buy that new car you've been eyeing. But believe you me, your all-knowing hubby will soon grow weary of your constant cries for help and over-whelming need for his attention. He will suddenly discover he now has another child on his hands.

This is pure joy, I tell you! I've done this dozens of times, and it gets more delightful each time because my husband doesn't even see it coming! When I ask for help (which I rarely do), he gets this glow in his eyes because he loves the fact that I need him, and he still serves a grand purpose on this earth. Co-dependency maneuvers work like a charm! Your hubby believes you're completely beholden to him, but the truth is he's just a puppet in your grand play and you've got the starring role.

This is how things go down:

Tell your man you feel overwhelmed, and request his help for even the smallest task. Since your man thinks so highly of himself (as most men do), he'll start taking over everything. Before you know it, your husband will be DOING IT ALL—the cooking, cleaning, schlepping, scheduling—and you'll get a much-deserved break! Hilarious, right? Remember girls, being a co-dependent can sometimes be *just* what the doctor ordered!

10 *Digitally Alter Your Wedding Photo*

Do you ever look at your wedding pictures and feel like you don't even know who that fresh-faced girl is anymore? We all know marriage has its ups and downs, but there's just something about your wedding day that seriously makes you the happiest woman on earth because you truly believe you've found the ideal man to share your life with and that every day will be just as happy as this! I smiled so much on my wedding day my cheeks literally ached at the end of the night, and I couldn't wait to get my pictures back so I could relive the joy over and over again. (Then I fast-forward twelve years and think, boy, was I living in dreamland!)

> **RISK INDICATOR: 1**
> *You're in the Clear*
> Even if your husband isn't thrilled with your new hobby, you'll have a blast—and if you're feeling generous, you can make supermodel Heidi Klum his digital bride.

After I'm done closely examining myself in the wedding photos, I take a long hard look at my husband's image and what a dashing groom he made. I remember it took him a whole hour to comb his hair that morning. He looks younger, of course, and definitely not the curmudgeon he sometimes turns into as we approach our forties. As I look at his picture I wonder what would have happened if fate had stepped in and another guy in a tux had been at my side. Would I look as happy?

Which brings me to the task at hand. For our tenth anniversary, I paid big money to have one of my color wedding photos reprinted in black and white as a gift for my husband. (He had wanted our entire wedding shot in black and white, but I nixed the idea, so I figured he'd appreciate the gesture.) The day I went to pick up the finished photo, I told the clerk there had been a mistake; Brad Pitt was supposed to be in the photo next to me, not my husband. He laughed, and said, "You have no idea how many women tell me the same thing!" This sparked a great idea: A digital "redo" of your wedding. It's really quite simple. Just scan a couple of your favorite shots, and with the right cut-and-paste program you could suddenly be married to Brad Pitt, Patrick Dempsey, Chris Noth (yummy Mr. Big from *Sex and The City*!), Denzel Washington, Johnny Depp, David Beckham (or any other of the male celebs who have graced the cover of *People*'s Sexiest Man Alive issue).

You can also go with your personal guy of choice. It doesn't have to be a celebrity—it could be your next-door neighbor if that tickles your fancy (celebs are just a bit safer unless you want to arouse major suspicion). But you get the point. Since we can't turn back the hands of time and actually marry someone else, this is the ideal remedy. I'm not sure he'll think it's a genius idea, but you should both be able to laugh about it—and the pics will always provide a smile whenever you need a little pick-me-up.

11 *Ruin His Day with Four Little Words "We need to talk."*

Nothing is worse than the gut-wrenching anxiety that comes with this very short but powerful sentence. No one likes to hear it, because positive information rarely follows that kind of declaration. Yep, dem's usually fightin' words—the beginning of a lengthy battle in which tears (and sometimes blood) are shed. Here's a scenario you can use as a guide should you choose this form of husband torture.

RISK INDICATOR: 1
You're in the Clear
Every woman is entitled to a bad day, right? And just in case he happens to flip out because the anxiety really got to him, you can always blame good ol' PMS.

Take your average Friday morning. Your husband is getting ready for work and seems to be in a happy mood because, as I said, it's Friday. As he's going about his morning business (shaving, combing his hair, brushing his teeth, etc.), you should pace around and make him feel generally uncomfortable, as if something is very wrong and you are disturbed and anguished about it. When he's almost done (and is maybe having breakfast or getting his things together moments before he heads out the door), just utter that simple sentence: "We need to talk." The immediate reaction to those dreaded words is usually a frozen state of panic. He suddenly can't move, and can barely breathe. His heart begins to pound, his palms may get sweaty, and he will very likely have a shocked expression on his face. "Um . . . is everything okay?" he might say. To which you answer, "No, everything is not okay, but we'll talk later, when you get home." The panic further increases and he could probably use a barf bag at that moment, although he's trying to keep his composure and not fall apart. "Okay sweetie . . . I'll be home at the usual time. Is there anything you want to tell me now?" he asks, fearing the answer. You reply, "Nope, I really don't want to ruin your day, honey, so go to work, and we'll talk later." Here's the thing: *His day has already been ruined.* Those four little words make quite an impact, and I assure you he'll be going insane for the next eight hours wondering what kind of monster issue he'll have to face when he gets home. His mind will start racing. He'll retrace his steps and think about what he may have done wrong in the past week or month; maybe you found his well-hidden porn stash, maybe you're angry at that comment he made a week ago about your hair looking funny. "Did she find out about my cyber-cheating?" He may wonder. "Oh my God—could she be pregnant?" "Does she want a divorce?"

The panic will set in faster than Super Glue and he'll be preoccupied all day imagining what monumental issue has to be dealt with. When he finally comes home (anxiously awaiting your discussion), just blow off the whole thing and tell him, "Oh honey, it was no big deal. I was just having a bad morning. Sorry!"

While it's very common for most people to deal with mild anxiety from time to time (especially those of us who've been married for more than a decade), the National Institute of Mental Health estimates about 19 million Americans suffer from anxiety disorders of some type, including panic attacks, social anxiety disorder, and posttraumatic stress disorder. Anxiety disorders occur equally in men and women, and heredity is often a contributing factor.

12 Clean Out His Crap

On the average, men don't appreciate anybody touching their stuff. However, they still leave it lying around everywhere and anywhere—and they actually get *pissy* when we complain. I guess they'd like us to make believe their dust-covered junk hogging up space and blocking doorways is simply invisible.

RISK INDICATOR: 3
He Might Be On to You
Getting a construction Dumpster beforehand would probably be a bit obvious. Wait till he's gone, and then let the removal begin!

But since we can't do that (and your friends aren't buyin' the "We're having a yard sale" excuse), solve this irritating junk dilemma by going on a mad cleaning spree. Let your urge to purge take over, randomly grab whatever you can get your hands on, and **toss it out the door!** Try as hard as you can to work around your man's schedule (i.e., aim for when he's at work or away with his buddies on one of those women-bashing guy weekends). Your little pack-rattin' beloved won't know what hit him when he gets home!

13 Threaten to Get Him in His Sleep

Trust is an interesting thing. It usually develops over time, with the mutual sharing of personal information about goals, fears, and secret dreams, and a deep belief that you can depend on each other come hell or high water.

> **RISK INDICATOR: 1**
> *You're in the Clear*
> Threatening sleep revenge is just a form of childish badgering, and it works to keep your man on his toes.

It is trust that led most of us to the altar, and it is trust that keeps us married. Trust is the foundation of all human relationships. If you ask married couples why they trust their mates they are most likely to say they trust so-and-so because "I can tell her anything," or because "he makes me feel happy and loved." I can honestly say I trust my husband because he's never done anything devious to me while I'm sleeping. Forget sharing our innermost thoughts and dreams, or even divulging our most private financial information—sleeping next to another human is by far the ultimate form of trust! There you are, completely vulnerable to practically anything (including major bouts of male flatulence) as you are deep in slumber. Every night we put our lives in the hands of our mates as we drift off to dreamland *hoping* to return to the world in the morning.

By trusting the person we share our bed with, we can all fall victim to anything—from a silly prank to being attacked in our sleep. So the

DON'T TRY THIS AT HOME!

From *The Tampa Times*, 2007.

A Florida woman is in jail after pouring hot grease on her sleeping husband. Police say Tampa resident Tanesha Young believed that her husband, Antone Neely, was having an affair. After an argument Monday night, Neely fell asleep in a chair. That's when Young allegedly poured the hot grease on his body, severely burning him. After seeking help at a neighbor's, Neely drove himself to a nearby hospital. Young was later found hiding in a closet at her mother's house and arrested.

next time your husband needs a dose of mental torture, say something subtly menacing like, "Just wait till you fall asleep; you have *no idea* what I could do to you." The fear will register immediately. No one likes the idea of falling asleep only to become prey, so scare the bejesus out of him and tell him you're gonna get him after he drifts off.

14 Pick a Fight During the Game

This is so entertaining it shouldn't even be allowed! There's nothing better than picking a fight with someone on purpose when they are completely caught off guard. I've become such an expert at picking fights

> **RISK INDICATOR: 2**
> *Caution, Girlfriend*
> Wearing protective headgear while picking a fight on game day is always a good idea, and hopefully you can make up at the end with a couple of touchdowns of your own.

that I even pick fights about picking fights, which is comedy at its highest level. Women generally pick fights with their mates when they have some built-up resentment or unresolved issue that needs to be addressed, RIGHT NOW. As intelligent women, we can admit we can become completely irrational when we're in "fight-picking" mode. Sometimes you don't even know it's coming—it just blows up and turns you into a raving lunatic in a millisecond. To illustrate, here's an example of unplanned fight-picking by an angry, irrational, possible hormonal female in a seething rage:

Him: "Hey babe, nice day, isn't it?"

Her: "I guess for *some people* it might be a nice day."

Him: "So what are we doing for lunch?"

Her: "I DON'T KNOW WHAT WE'RE DOING FOR LUNCH!! WHY DO I HAVE TO HAVE ALL THE ANSWERS?? I KNEW FROM THE MINUTE I MARRIED YOU THAT YOU WERE A COMPLETE IDIOT!! AND I THINK SEAFOAM GREEN IS A BETTER COLOR FOR THE LIVING ROOM NO MATTER WHAT YOUR MOTHER THINKS!!!"

There you go, a prime example of fight-picking, and we've all done it consciously or subconsciously at some point in our relationship. Because we are such expert fight-pickers, there's no better way to torture a sports-obsessed male than to stage a massive throwdown just as he's getting ready to enjoy his favorite sport, nestled in his favorite chair, with his favorite beverage and nosh at his side. Go ahead and let him get settled, then make your move. The best time to do this, of course, is when his favorite team is playing a deciding game that will lead them to the playoffs, or when Tiger Woods is getting ready to win some other award for being the greatest golfer in the universe, when the Mets and Yankees are in the middle of a Subway Series, or any other major sporting event that bores you to tears but is your man's greatest reason for living.

PROOF POSITIVE

According to the *World Encyclopedia*, soccer is the most popular international team sport, with about 3.5 billion fans worldwide. Brazil's Pele is considered the best soccer player who ever lived. His real name is Edson Arantes do Nascimento. He scored 1,281 goals in 1,363 games and went to the World Cup three times before retiring in 1977, making way for soccer greats such as England's David Beckham, Germany's Franz Beckenbauer, Argentina's Diego Maradona, and France's Zinadine Zidane. Despite soccer's international popularity, it has long been secondary in the United States, where American football, a descendant of rugby, continues to dominate.

Because tensions are so high, picking a fight before a big game is as easy as scalping tickets at Fenway Park—you don't have to try too hard. Just standing in front of the TV should be enough, but if you really want to get crazy, let your husband get comfy, take his first swig of beer, and then request his undivided attention to discuss some trivial issue like what to get your mom for her birthday. He'll try to blow you off and say something like, "Not now honey, I'm watching the game." Your response should be as drama-filled as possible ("YOU NEVER HELP ME WHEN I NEED YOU!!"), and just take it from there. You should definitely be able to stretch out the fight until he's at least missed a couple of innings. Heck, if you milk it, the entire game might be over before you know it!

15 Tell Him His Dad Is Hot

WARNING: *The following subject matter is somewhat disturbing and may cause any or all of the following symptoms: severe nausea, sudden rash, violent shudders, joint pain, swelling, split personality disorder, night sweats, bowel disturbances, thoughts of suicide, and a strong desire to gouge out your eyes. Proceed at your own risk!*

> **RISK INDICATOR: 4**
> **Watch Your Back**
> While this exercise might work, your husband might decide to retaliate and develop his own sick fantasy about your mom. Keep your therapist's number handy.

I am a lucky girl. I happen to have a great relationship with my father-in-law. We both love ice cream, a good joke, spontaneous naps, and he can entertain my son for hours making paper airplanes and reading passages from the latest edition of *Hot Wheels* magazine. My father-in-law kind of looks like Buddy Holly, especially in his wedding picture. That's my favorite picture of him because he was a hottie back then. I made the mistake of sharing that thought with my husband one afternoon while we were sifting through old photos. Now, let me make this abundantly clear: I might have a pretty wild imagination and I get a kick out of breaking stupid rules and raising hell on occasion, but I could never fathom in a million years thinking about my father-in-law in a sexual way. The "hottie" comment just slipped out as I examined the old wedding photo that day, but you should have seen the look on my husband's face! I thought his eyes were going to burst right out of their sockets! And the offending remark has been a source of deep trauma ever since. We're talking irreparable mental damage. But it's turned out for the best because I know whenever I want to make my husband sick to his stomach and inflict a strong dose of torture, I only have to make the slightest reference about his dad being attractive. So if you really want to screw up your husband mentally and send him straight to therapy, tell him you're "crushing" on his dad. The more you elaborate on the topic, the more torture you will inflict. And I assure you the reaction you will get is absolutely **priceless**.

16 *Creep Him Out by Being Extra Nice*

We're not so kind to our husbands for a mind-boggling myriad of reasons. It could be that he just did something wrong; it could be that we're still holding a grudge about something annoying he did back in 1998; or you might be angry about something he hasn't even done yet but is already chafing your ass! The fact

> **RISK INDICATOR: 2**
> *Caution, Girlfriend*
> He could quickly get used to the kindness, which we all know ain't sticking around for long!

is, husbands start off with a clean slate and before you know it, they become that annoying pebble in your shoe.

I truly believe (and I'm no scientist here) that all men are born without a very necessary gene. Let's call it the "awareness gene." Men are blissfully unaware of many things that happen around them. The awareness gene would keep a man out of a massive amount of trouble—they would never make clueless mistakes and their marriages would be a whole lot more pleasant! This lack of awareness naturally forces us to be total bitches (something most husbands are **used to)**, so suddenly being extra *nice* will scare them to death and send them running for the hills. Let's practice these key phrases you can use . . . without any trace of sarcasm, which might be difficult:

- "Sweetie, I made your favorite dinner . . . and we can have dessert later (wink, wink)."
- "You know, I should listen to you more often because you are *always right*!"
- "No, let me take the garbage out, you've worked too hard today."
- "Honey, where would I be without you?"
- "Hey, how 'bout I treat you to a massage while you're watching the game?"

Believe me, after a few days of this kind of sickly-sweet treatment, he'll be begging you to be mean to him again!

17 "Quit" Your Job

C'mon, you know you're not so fond of that hellish place you call work anyhow, and what a way to really make your hubby's ass burn! You may have dreamt of quitting for weeks, months—even years. You might loathe your boss, it could be your coworkers, or you've just been there so long you've become a permanent fixture like the wallpaper on the wall. My philosophy is, when you're really miserable in a dead-end job (and even the not-so-dead-end jobs), any time is a good time to file for "fun-employment" and move on to something better, or just stay home and see all the inter-

> **RISK INDICATOR: 2**
> *Caution, Girlfriend*
> Once you become successfully "fun-employed" you might end up working harder than you ever thought. Your husband will soon be asking you to run his errands, andyou will find yourself doing "busywork" around the house just to stay sane. Plus, being a stay-at-home mom is no walk in the park, so be advised.

esting stuff you miss while you're at work (like the neighbor who's apparently running a small-scale gambling ring, or the smokin' hot UPS deliveryman who leaves packages at your door).

Here's how you get the job done. Just head to your place of employment on a regular noneventful morning, have your coffee, pretend to work, enjoy an extended lunch hour with your closest coworkers, turn in that final paperwork, then look your annoying boss dead in the eye and say "You are an asshole. And by the way, today is my last day!" What a RUSH!! Once you've been escorted out of the building by security, head to the nearest liquor establishment and pick up an ultra-expensive bottle of bubbly. After getting home and slipping into your new work attire (a.k.a. your jammies), let the alcohol flow and let your husband in on the big news! "Honey, I quit my job! I'm finally freeeee!" (Dancing in your underwear while setting the company manual on fire is perfectly acceptable as well.) Your husband's jaw will drop. He'll be flabbergasted, he'll wonder what demons have possessed you, and he'll definitely want to know how much you really spent on that damn champagne. After tackling a bewildering questioning session at the hands of your very confused husband, assure him that this is just a temporary situation. Make him understand that you only quit because you were so unhappy, and you know you can find an even BETTER job now that you are free of all the negativity and depression. Tell him that you fully intend to find gainful employment again, how you LOVE being overworked and underappreciated, and how you would NEVER want to stay home and allow your brain to turn to mush (I mean, who would want to do that?). Promise him that it will never happen again, and proceed to spend the next days, weeks, months, and maybe even years "hitting the pavement" ACTING like you are wholeheartedly looking for a new gig while doing absolutely the opposite.

Of course, if you're not in a financial position to quit your job, don't tell your boss where to shove it, but you can still make your hubby THINK you did, which is almost more delicious! Start with the bubbly and jammies portion of this trick, and after you watch the color drain from your beloved's face, and enjoy the sight of him stressing to the point of hyperventilating, lay a big ole "PSYCH!" on him. Works every time!

18 *Have Lunch with Your Ex*

Why is it that any contact with an ex-boyfriend will immediately turn a husband into a juggernaut of jealousy? Men should know that many women keep their exes around as a silly form of masochism (or to make sure that racy video doesn't end up on YouTube), but hanging out with your ex is a surefire

> **RISK INDICATOR: 4**
> *Watch Your Back*
> Your husband may resort to all kinds of mayhem to keep this lunch date from happening, so stay on your toes.

way of torturing a husband because he has *no control whatsoever*—and that makes him crazier than Mel Gibson on a bender! However, a very important tip is to not disclose your plans too far in advance. Take it from a seasoned pro. My husband is well aware of the fact that I keep in touch with a couple of my old flames. It doesn't it matter that I find most of them utterly repulsive now. I keep them around for ammunition. You never know when one of these stupid jerks from your past will come in handy to make your hubby insanely jealous. As I said, even though my husband knows I have sporadic conversations (text messages, e-mails, etc.) with some of my exes, he still gets bent out of shape when I casually say, "Oh, I forgot to tell you I'm having lunch with Sam tomorrow. He's working on a new project and wants to tell me about it." No matter what he's doing, when my husband hears

DON'T TRY THIS AT HOME!

From the *Yorkshire Post*, March 2008.

A jealous husband who tried to kill his wife after becoming convinced she had an affair has been jailed for 18 years. Ricky Walker, 41, told his wife Cheryl, 38, that "she was going to die for it" before shooting her twice at close range with an air rifle. He then turned the gun on himself, but failed to commit suicide. The pair had been married for years but prosecutors say Walker became "consumed with jealousy" after his wife innocently helped a man stranded in a flood last year. Investigating officer, Detective Sergeant Paul Walker said: "This was a planned and violent attack, based on Walker's paranoia and unfounded jealousy." Luckily, Mrs. Walker survived the attack.

those words he stops dead in his tracks and gives me one of his "I don't approve" looks (that I pretend to not see) and the torture is ON.

Sometimes he might have a follow-up question, like "Where are you guys going on this lunch date you hadn't told me about?" WARNING: This is a trap! Do not provide any further info, for it may be used against you! Always answer the follow-up question with, "I'm not sure yet, he's e-mailing me in the morning." This guarantees your safety—at least for now. (I once told my husband where I was meeting an ex for lunch, and guess who decided to show up for a bite? Yep. There I was sitting with my husband and my ex at the same table—and they happened to get along famously! That was a major mistake on my part, so don't let it happen to you.) You must maintain utmost secrecy to achieve the best torture. Done right, your husband will feel extremely jealous and threatened by this blast from your past, something *all men* loathe. Don't worry, you'll put his fears to rest later on. You honestly don't even have to break bread with your ex to put your husband on edge. You can make the whole thing up if you really want to be cruel, and once he gets all worked up you can let him in on your little secret, which will make him feel like a total ass. Meeting for coffee (or any beverage for that matter) is also acceptable and less time consuming than lunch. It is all up to you, girlfriend. You hold the cards, so dish out as much torture as you see fit!

19 Tell Him the Truth When He Gets You a Stupid Present

Every woman deserves a shiny Academy Award (or two) for acting her socks off every time she receives a painfully dull present like a DustBuster, wall clock, or matronly nightgown. I mean seriously, what are men thinking when they go to the store? It's like a sick joke when they do this kind of stuff, and I could never for the life of me understand

> **RISK INDICATOR: 1**
> *You're in the Clear*
> After all the disappointing gift episodes you've endured, your man totally deserves a wake-up call, and it will force him to actually "think" before his next present purchase!

what possesses them to make such painfully wrong choices! Cut to an average man's thought process as he enters the mall searching for the perfect gift to present to his loving wife: "Hmm. Let's see. Over here there's fantastic jewelry in all shapes and sizes, the latest in fashionable female attire (and deliciously sexy lingerie), designer footwear, the latest in name-brand makeup, a plethora of purses and pricey accessories, and fragrances to captivate every one of my senses. Nah. I'm not sure any of that will work. BUT WAIT. Oh yes. I've hit the JACKPOT! I am going to make a most remarkable purchase today. I have found THE present I've been looking for! My wife is going to swoon the very second she opens this box and feasts her eyes on this incredible, high-tech, delightfully colorful, aerodynamic, awe-inspiring, multifaceted IRON."

It's like getting kicked straight in the stomach. Obviously, the answer here is that men aren't thinking when they buy inane gifts, so why should we make them feel like they've brought home some great prize and actually reward them for being so unbelievably clueless? This is another instance when "faking it" just doesn't pay off, ladies. But we've all done it, right? We've all received a gift that has made us shudder (in a bad way), yet we immediately turn on the charm to protect our man's emotions:

"Oh gosh. (Very long pause.) Thanks. (Another very long pause.) Thank you SO much honey, I've been eyeing this iron for months! It's perfect, and I CAN'T WAIT to use it! In fact, I'll start right now! I've got a mountain of ironing to do, so plug it in baby! This is the best present in the HISTORY of presents! I'm the luckiest woman alive!"

Let's put an end to this charade. The gig is officially up. The next time your man gets you a thoughtless, inappropriate, or downright crappy gift, forget about his fragile feelings and tell him you absolutely HATE IT. How many times have you thought there could be a sparkly diamond necklace in that long little box, and it turns out to be a friggin' pen? Enough with the girlish manners! Tell him how you really feel in detail, and after an extended amount of pouting, I'm sure your husband will finally see the light and realize the error of his ways. To really send the right message, make him return the offending present and purchase something acceptable. The return process should continue until he finally gets it right.

DON'T TRY THIS AT HOME!

From *AP News*, Rock Springs, Wyoming, December 22, 2007. A woman stabbed her husband with a kitchen knife following an argument that began when she accused him of opening a Christmas present too early. Thirty-four-year-old Misty Johnson was arrested and charged with aggravated assault and battery, a felony, and misdemeanor domestic battery. Her husband, Shawn Fay Johnson, also 34, was treated at a hospital for a wound to the chest.

Chapter Two

PHYSICAL TORTURE

20 *Attack Him with a Nerf Bat*

Sometimes I would love to use a real bat and score some excellent RBI's (or break one of my husband's R-I-B's), but doing prison time is not an item on my "to-do list," so here's an entertaining alternative. Blow off enormous loads of steam by borrowing your kid's sturdy Nerf bat or pick one up at your local toy store, and get ready for some major league action! At this moment I'm wondering if baseball

RISK INDICATOR: 4
Watch Your Back
He may not take this too well, and what's worse is that he may retaliate when you least expect it. But it's still worth the risk as far as I'm concerned!

superstars like Derek Jeter, Cal Ripken Jr., and A-Rod (who is such a hottie) found their true calling on that fateful day when they picked up their very first Nerf bat and felt that rush you can only feel when you know you're about to open a serious can of whup-ass on one of your nearest and dearest friends or family members. The rush only increases when your victim is down and you keep pounding him until some annoying "do-gooder" puts an end to your adrenaline-filled assault. We have to hand it to the company that created this genius product—where would we be without the aggression Nerf has helped us all unleash?

You see, a bit of "kind hurting" goes a long way. It shows your zest for fun and cruelty all at the same time, which is what this exercise is all about. The surprise element is really important here; you'll want to make sure your guy doesn't see it coming. Wait for it . . . and then BAM! I'll tell ya, it's the best kind of stress relief a couple of bucks can buy, and those who had sadistic siblings like I did know that a Nerf bat can definitely provide some bruising if used appropriately! Your husband will obviously try to shield himself, but he'll think you're just being playful and will probably let you get some good shots in. Of course, this is when you should really let him have it. He won't even know what to do with himself!

21 Bribe Him with Sex—Don't Pay Up!

Q: Why was the bride smiling as she walked down the aisle?

A: Because she knows she's given her last blow job!

I really never got this joke—until I got married. I don't care what anybody says, sex generally dies down after marriage, and there's nothing you can do about it. It's just part of the marriage deception we all fall for. You sincerely believe if you're married, and living under the same roof, you just won't be able to keep

> **RISK INDICATOR: 4**
> *Watch Your Back*
> Withholding sex from a man is like taunting a hungry tiger. He might pounce at any second.

your hands off each other, and you can have sex at any moment. But that's precisely what ruins it.

You know why we look forward to having funnel cakes at the fair? Because the fair, and the funnel cakes, only come around once or twice a year! So you look forward to it, and can't wait to sink your teeth into one. On the flip side, if you could have funnel cakes every day, here's what would transpire over time: Upon hearing that you could enjoy a sweet, greasy funnel cake on a daily basis, you would squeal with excitement and gobble up that baby in a second. After weeks of daily funnel-cake eating, your passion for the treat would start to fade. You might still enjoy them, but much less than you used to. Months later you find yourself coming up with creative ways to make that funnel cake appetizing again. You sprinkle it with cinnamon, chocolate powder, or even paprika because you are so bored with the taste you could scream. At this point, you begin to wonder why you ever liked funnel cakes so much in the first place! A year later the love affair is officially over. You have now come to detest funnel cakes and will come up with any reason to avoid eating that loathsome fried batter!

Same goes for sex.

Sex is great, but the monotony of marriage tends to stifle it, so that's why men can be lured by the bribing maneuver so easily. First, you must withhold intimacy for at least two weeks (should be simple, since married people are lucky if they do it once a month). Since your hubby is probably already on a "sex fast," he'll be thrilled by the prospect of getting some, so this is when you make your offer, which goes something like this: "Okay, honey. We can have sex tonight if you do the laundry, or mow the lawn (or do whatever it is you want him to do)." Your man will immediately agree, and get the appointed chore done lickety-split, all because you've given him sex as a magnificent incentive. Sure, he doesn't know you don't intend on paying your bill just yet, and will make him suffer for a few more days just to mess with his mind, but that's the thrill of it! When he comes around looking to "collect," tell him the office is closed for the evening, and he'll have to try back tomorrow. Kick the torture up a notch by wearing racy lingerie to bed, but sleeping soundly all night long.

22 *Sign Him Up for a Dance Class*

Look out *Dancing with the Stars*! Mooooove over Deney Terrio. Here's a way to leave your husband severely dazed, breathless, and consequently very confused. Break out your dancin' shoes and get ready for some rump sha-kin', earth quaking, sweat-till-you-drop kind of torture—the kind only new pat-ent leather tap shoes can provide!

RISK INDICATOR: 1
You're in the Clear
He may initially hate you for signing up for dance demen-tia, but he'll thank you later when he can show off his enviable moves.

Face it: except for a select handful of men throughout history (Fred Astaire, Mikhail Baryshnikov, Gene Kelly, Gregory Hines, for exam-ple), the stereotypical "manly man" generally doesn't enjoy the art of dance, is turned off by the idea of unleashing his inhibitions, pranc-ing around in tights (or revealing, shiny, sequined-covered clothing), and letting his body groove to the music. Most men think dancing is a "feminine" kind of thing, and rarely hit a dance floor unless they are forced by a nagging, persistent, ultra-demanding force in their lives: their wife. Think of countless weddings where the dance floor is taken over by that wild, tumbleweed-like throng of tipsy, overheated women gyrating together as they delightedly sing along to some ancient ABBA tune, and dance the night away without the company of any men whatsoever. At some point the women got tired of begging their significant others to join them and decided to ditch their heels and boogie down with fellow "Dancing Queens" while the severely uncoordinated husbands sit silently at their respective tables and get shit-faced on the free alcohol!

In the name of torture and for all the times we've been discarded on the dance floor, tackling your man's two left feet will be a divine enterprise, and there's only one way to go about it: Don't say a word, find the most reputable dance studio in your area, and sign up for at least eight weeks of excruciatingly difficult dance instruction. He'll have to comply when he finds out you've also paid in advance and there are no refunds. (Listen, you feed him that line whether it's true or not; otherwise, he won't show up!)

When it comes to deciding on whether you'd like to have private lessons or learn in a group setting, I would advise you to go with the group class for a variety of reasons. The risk of public embarrassment for him will be greater, but he'll also have other males around to bond with, which will hopefully keep him from bailing on you before the second class! A group class can also provide plenty of laughter therapy when you witness other couples bickering about who stepped on whose toes, and constant heated discussions about foot placement and proper form.

There are so many wonderful styles to choose from . . . action-packed swing, treacherous tap, boring ballroom, stroke-inducing salsa, hip-breaking hip-hop, or cringe-worthy country western! Check out one or all! Just keep a defibrillator handy, because you just might tango, hustle, and rumba him all the way to the emergency room.

PROOF POSITIVE

According to TV.com, before television audiences were dazzled by performance-based reality shows like *Dancing with the Stars* and *So You Think You Can Dance*, America suffered from a scorching case of *Dance Fever*! This syndicated musical variety series made its debut in 1979 and concluded in 1987. It was created and produced by Merv Griffin and hosted by actor Deney Terrio. The show featured amateur dancers, celebrity judges, and performances from top pop, disco, and R&B artists.

23 Lock Him Out in a Storm

No one likes to get caught in unpleasant weather. This torture technique actually occurred to me one frigid afternoon on Long Island as we were hunkered down waiting for a nasty Nor'easter to blast the region with dangerous winds and blanket it with more than two feet of snow. The atmosphere was fierce and that foreboding storm vibe caused panic to slowly seep in. "Do we have everything we need if we're snowed

> **RISK INDICATOR: 1**
> *You're in the Clear*
> Mistakes happen, don't they? Be a good actress and he'll be none the wiser. Remember: drinking hot chocolate by the window while watching him squirm would be fun, but is not advisable.

in?" I wondered to myself as hail smacked the roof above. I held my infant son just a little closer. High winds were kicking up, battering the enormous holly tree on our front lawn. My husband (who was acting like a nervous poodle awaiting impending doom) told me he was heading outside to "batten down the hatches," and make sure everything was tied down, nailed down, or otherwise secure. I appreciated his overly cautious behavior, but I was suddenly annoyed. While my husband had been at work that day, I had already seen to all that! I took the time to empty my son's neglected algae-filled kiddie pool. I had already stacked the lawn chairs and placed them in the shed. I even battled a large brown spider who was pretty pissed when I took down the picnic table umbrella. This was going to be a monster storm, after all, and I wanted to be prepared (even if I ruined my newly salon-coiffed hair in the freezing rain!). Once my husband arrived, I assured him we were ready. At the very least I expected an approving high-five or a confident nod. But instead, what did I get? Insecurity and doubt. (My husband obviously thinks I am incapable of storing lawn furniture properly!) So you can guess what happened next. Upon his exit into the frozen back yard, I locked the door, put my son down for a nap, and took a long, hot shower. About an hour later I emerged to find my husband peering angrily though the sliding glass door begging for re-entry. I hurried to the door and began apologizing immediately. (I was suddenly thankful I took those three acting classes in college, 'cause my performance actually convinced my husband it was all just a big mistake! Inside I was laughing triumphantly.)

So take your pick: Snowstorm, rainstorm, hailstorm, tropical storm, hurricane, tornado, tempest, blizzard, squall, windstorm, thunderstorm, tropical disturbance, tsunami, typhoon, blazing sun. Whatever you choose will work as long as you make him *truly believe* it was a mistake.

24 Do Some "Man-Scaping"

I always wonder: If women had the choice to become men overnight, how many would take the offer? I mean I love being a woman, but imagine suddenly not needing to do all the primping and upkeep that comes along when you are born with two X chromosomes! It's so easy being a male, and I'm

RISK INDICATOR: 5
Run Like Hell
Man-scaping is never a pain-free process. He'll get used to it eventually, but keep a healthy distance at first.

not talking about this on an emotional level, just the level of simple maintenance.

Here's the average man's day: Shower, brush teeth, comb hair (optional), put clothes on, head to work.

Here's the average woman's day: Wake up with caked-on rejuvenating wrinkle cream from previous night. Brush teeth with whitening-power toothpaste, pluck eyebrows, check to see if the "chickstache" (female mustache) is growing back and needs waxing. No? Good. Proceed to check your weight on the scale. Vicious screams are heard clear across town as you realize you are now up three pounds despite the fact that you've only had carrots for eight consecutive days. Once in the shower, slather watermelon exfoliating scrub all over to ensure glowing skin, and suffer painful nicks while shaving legs, underarms, and possibly "vajayjay" if time allows. Once "hair-free" and squeaky-clean, comb your hair, realize you need to see colorist, and move on to the closet to choose an outfit for the day. Nothing is acceptable (because of the extra three pounds, of course) so squeeze into extremely uncomfortable dress pants and a tight-fitting blouse, which will compromise breathing for the rest of the day, leaving coworkers to wonder if the asthma or labored breathing is due to the extremely tight and unflattering wardrobe obviously favored.

The bottom line? Being a woman (or at least a well-coiffed one) requires work.

So how do we get even?

Convince your husband he needs some meticulous "man-scaping" to look his very best. If you tell him you'd probably have more sex with him if he waxes his chest, he'll be booking an appointment that same day! As you know, waxing can be done in all areas where hair grows, including his arms, eyebrows, legs, and the pelvic "love trail." Being around for that will be priceless, so take time off of work if you must to enjoy the show! Full-body wax is recommended. Not only is extensive waxing excruciatingly painful, but he won't be leaving yucky hairs on the bathroom floor anymore (hallelujah!).

Other "man-scaping" ideas include getting a facial. But we're not talking the relaxing "spa kind," more like the "make you cry like a new-born EXTRACTION FACIAL." That's where an aesthetician removes gross stuff like blackheads, whiteheads, and pimples from facial pores (while making you clench your spa table in wincing pain).

Manicures and pedicures aren't necessarily painful, but men loathe the idea of being seen in one of these places, surrounded by chatty women. So that brings me to this point:

If your husband refuses to get any man-scaping done at the hands of a professional, don't give up. If you offer like a broken record to do it personally for him, he'll be running in the direction of the spa in no time. He knows that with the professionals he's in better hands—who knows what you'll do to him, given the chance!

25 Add Laxatives to His Dinner

This exercise is the perfect revenge for those hard-to-please husbands who constantly complain about the meal you just slaved over for hours and show no appreciation whatsoever for your time-consuming effort! In my mind, anyone who cooks a meal for you (be it your mom, friend, insignificant family member, neighbor, or complete stranger) should become a personal hero. I know my standards are low, but it should be evident by now that cooking is as foreign as car repair to me, so I think *very* highly of anyone who not only prepares an entire meal, but does so in my honor! That's why I take such offense to criticism when it comes to my cooking. I know it doesn't have Emeril Lagasse's seal of approval, but at least be kind enough to not spit out your mouthful until I'm not looking! (And if you're reading, hubby, take note that telling me what ingredients you would add or avoid next time doesn't help either!) Now, if you happen to be one of those Martha Stewart types who can whip up delicacies

> **RISK INDICATOR: 2**
> *Caution, Girlfriend*
> You'll probably get away with it and laugh about it for years, but don't get cocky and try this too often. Your guy will inevitably catch on, putting an end to your cooking cruelties faster than you can say "pass the Alka-Seltzer."

DON'T TRY THIS AT HOME!

Cheltenham, England, May 28, 2008 (UPI via COMTEX)

A British woman avoided prison time after a judge decided she wasn't "seeing things straight" when she baked rat poison into a cake for her husband. Judge Jamie Tabor ruled former chef Yvonne Godwin, 56, was not a "criminal in any shape or form" because she turned herself in for putting a teaspoon of rat poison in her husband's food to "stop him leaving the house to see his mistress," the *Daily Mail* reported. Godwin claimed she was recovering from cancer and driven to the edge when she found out her abusive husband of 30 years, Robert Godwin, 63, was cheating on her with the sister of her close friend.

in mere moments with one hand tied behind your perfectly tied apron, lucky you . . . this exercise will be as easy as peach pie!

Execution: Prepare one of his favorite meals so he thinks you are trying really hard to impress him and make him happy. The meal you choose, though, is very important, because it should help to disguise the "special secret ingredient" you'll be adding during the cooking process. I would go with something meaty, and possibly featuring a hearty tomato-based sauce because you can't go wrong with that! After the magical meal has been decided, it's on to laxative options. Note that laxatives are not all created equal; some are chewable, others come in a time-release form that can take hours to work, while others are what I like to call "tummy-busters" and go to work immediately, often causing painful cramps and an urgent need to visit the boys' room! (Remember that hilarious bathroom scene in the movie *Dumb and Dumber*? It's remarkably realistic!) Whichever laxative you choose, just keep an eye out for the symptoms. They will come, and you can watch him writhing in pain as the magic ingredient starts to work—sometimes just minutes after the first mouthful!

WARNING: Don't overdo it! Read the laxative directions very carefully; after all, you don't want to end up making your husband really sick, which means *you'd* have to take care of *him!* There's nothing worse than a sick man. No matter what they have, they will swear they're dying and become infants, requesting assistance 24/7. So for optimal results, make sure to choose wisely and above all, destroy all evidence! Leaving the bright blue milk of magnesia bottle on the counter will not lead to a pleasant conversation. Good luck, and *bon appétit*!

26 *Nair His Hair*

Did you ever get a creamy hair removal product where you didn't mean to? Not a pretty sight . . . and sistahgirl, let's not even *talk* about getting that gunk in your eyes. Makes you want to gouge them out with a nail file! Now

RISK INDICATOR: 5
Run Like Hell
It's a hair-raising experience, but worth whatever retaliation is coming to you.

I know this is a silly collegiate prank, but it is definitely memorable, which is why it's still quite popular on or off college campuses. This means of torture is inexpensive, but long-lasting, which makes it one of my all-time favorites.

Act normal, calmly wait for your husband to fall into a deep slumber, and pounce! Ideally, your guy will be heavily intoxicated (say after downing a full bottle of vodka at his thirtieth birthday party?). Once you are absolutely sure the victim is out cold, break out your favorite hair remover—Neet, Veet, Nair, or Nad's will all work equally well. You know the cream-based products usually sting when they set, so your man will wake up in quite a huff (getting this on video will really add to the fun). Apply liberally to the face, legs, arms, chest, or wherever hair is present. (I tested out this sinister plan years ago on my poor friend Brandon, who was sleeping in the buff when I redecorated his privates!) Trust me, your husband WILL vow revenge.

27 Demand a Vasectomy

Does any man like the idea of someone tinkering with his nuts and bolts? The answer is a resounding "NO," but I'd like to thank whoever came up with the concept, because it's genius! Why do I feel this way? Well, before I had my son, I thought vasectomies were cruel and unusual punishment for a man, because after all, there are other forms of contraception and means of

RISK INDICATOR: 1
You're in the Clear
You can lead a man to a urologist, but you can't force him to get clipped. Keep on demanding it, though, and don't take no for an answer. He might eventually give in.

avoiding pregnancy. However, now that I've had my son and lived through the pain of childbirth, I think vasectomies are the ultimate form of payback—although we're still not entirely even in the end, frankly.

Ponder this: Women endure nine months of sheer discomfort, dealing with nausea, painful gas, weight gain, dizziness, stretch marks, constipation, countless doctor's appointments, poking, prodding, tests, stress, bloating, bladder dysfunctions, sleepless nights, heartburn, bizarre swelling, shortness of breath, back pain, gut-wrenching contractions, gargantuan breasts, and the constant fatigue brought on by the tiny human living in our uterus. And if that weren't enough, the arduous adventure culminates in the final moment where you propel the tiny human from your body with such intensity it permanently alters your mind, body, and soul. On the other hand, men get away with a simple outpatient procedure and a bag of ice for their balls. Definitely not even. Not remotely. But we'll take it. At least there's *something* we can get men to do for all our trouble.

So what does a vasectomy entail? An article in *Men's Health* describes the procedure: "Vasectomy is a surgical procedure during which the vas deferens—the tubes that carry sperm from the testes—are severed. Vasectomy is a very safe and permanent means of male contraception, though it can be reversed should the need arise. A vasectomy is a relatively quick procedure that takes about 30 minutes and is performed using a local anesthetic. The vas deferens are operated on one at a time. A very small incision is made and the tube is cut then sutured, cauterized, or clipped, in order to close them off.

After the procedure a man can go home the same day and be back to work within two or three days."

Pretty simple, right? Well, believe me, it's enough to give men nightmares. You can start by proposing the idea in the right setting, for example when you're having a romantic dinner and he thinks he's gonna get lucky. Catch him off-guard and just blurt it out. He'll be stunned and might even choke on his asparagus.

28 Booby-trap Your Home

DISCLAIMER: *The following section should only be considered in a fantasy scenario. My attorneys (a.k.a. pains in the butt) highly advise against suggesting such means of torture, so please stick to less physically harmful strategies, instead.*

> **RISK INDICATOR: 2**
> *Caution, Girlfriend*
> Stay sharp and remember the booby-traps you've set, or you could end up being the victim instead!

It wasn't on purpose. It *really* was an accident. I sprayed this thick, white sudsy cleanser all over my bathtub, and my husband slipped and fell. Hard. Really hard. Like a fat kid on the playground hard. I was home when it happened, and knew what had transpired the second I heard the helpless yelp followed by the loud KA-THUNK! I jumped up, ran to the bathroom, and found my naked husband fumbling on his back, covered in white foam from head to toe, unsuccessfully trying to grab on to something to get up. Of course I was concerned, but I couldn't keep myself from giggling while I extended my arms to get him on his feet. He was relieved I came to his aid, but incredibly furious that I had failed to warn him about the slippery bathroom situation. I was merely letting the cleanser work its magic (loosening up the dirt, and so forth) but after an hour or so, I had forgotten I even sprayed that stuff all over the bathtub! I knew I would eventually get around to cleaning the bathroom later on, but obviously my hubby beat me to it, and he had bruises all over his backside to prove it. I could just hear my mom's disapproving voice: "You have to be more careful dear, that's how accidents happen," but who could have foreseen the dangerous event? Upon doing some "accidental fall" research, I made a startling discovery. According to the National Safety Council, more than nine million disabling slip and fall injuries occur per year (luckily, my husband wasn't disabled, just angry). And that's how I came up with the plan.

You can get a mischievous kick out of setting up crafty booby-traps around the house, and making them *look like* accidents. Provided your children aren't around to fall prey, there are several things you can try to give your man a good scare, and possibly more if you're creative. How many times have you opened a closet door and gotten smacked in the head by a falling shoebox, or been buried under a sudden and violent clothes avalanche? Well, you can make it happen by simply loosening the shelf screws, or if you don't want to go to such drastic measures, simply position well-chosen items along shelf edges so they will no doubt come tumbling down the next time your man opens the door. Here's something else you can try: Heavily wax your floors and conveniently forget to tell your hubby about it, or leave spilled water in a strategic spot where he will most likely stampede through and find himself on his rear. Renegade area rugs are also a convenient prop for slipping and tripping (try folding a corner or causing a bump in the middle). And finally, leaving shoes strewn about or toys on stairs will definitely yield the desired result, and you can never be accused of setting the trap.

29 *Treat Him to a Massage (with a Male Masseuse!)*

I know few men who consistently go for massages (and I have an inkling it's because they'd rather not be naked unless there's an orgasm attached somehow) so they miss out on the sheer bliss of regular relaxing rubdowns—which bring you as close to heaven as you can possibly get without actually dying. Men might get a massage for a special occasion, say if

> **RISK INDICATOR: 1**
> *You're in the Clear*
> Expect your husband to complain about his unpleasant "manly" experience, but passive-aggressively remind him you were only trying to do something nice.

they happen to be on vacation, or maybe if they're suffering from some shoulder or back pain and they think it might help ease their discomfort. Sure, these scenarios are plausible, but if you ask any man the one prerequisite to getting a massage, they all come up with the same answer: a female masseuse. Well, you can definitely supply the massage (and the strong hands part) by booking your husband a full-body massage at your local spa with a large and extra-manly male massage specialist who will be happy to stroke and knead hubby's troubles away on the massage table. (Call ahead and place your special request with your spa of choice. Specify that there can be no last-minute changes, and mention there's a fat tip involved!) Of course, there are many massages to choose from, but I recommend deep-tissue or Shiatsu/Thai massage. Deep-tissue provides plenty of skin-on-skin friction with lots of pressure, and possible soreness afterward. Shiatsu/Thai both involve plenty of rhythmic touching (which your hubby will no doubt love), but when it comes to Thai massage, the therapist also moves your limbs about and stretches you in a series of postures that are awkward, and somewhat revealing and personal. (Can you imagine what will be going through your husband's mind while he's literally being man-handled?) You can also meet beforehand with the massage therapist and let him know your husband would prefer soothing, romantic music and very dim lights during his session. If you'd like, you can also throw in a facial for plenty of face-to-face male interaction he'll never forget. Go for broke on this one.

30 *Put Him on a Drastic Diet*

I'm on this new diet. Well, I don't eat anything, and when I feel like I'm about to faint, I eat a cube of cheese.—ACTRESS EMILY BLUNT, IN THE CHARACTER OF EMILY FROM THE MOVIE *THE DEVIL WEARS PRADA*

If there's one thing women know about, it's dieting. We've done them all, right? The Cabbage Soup Diet, the Green

> **RISK INDICATOR: 2**
> *Caution, Girlfriend*
> Putting a man on a diet is much like offering cocaine to Robert Downey Jr. He will eventually lose all control, go buck wild, and inhale everything in sight!

Tea Diet, vegan, no carbs, only carbs, colonics, the Cookie Diet, prescription pills, the "Orange Items" Diet, constipation-inducing protein bars, the Water Only Diet, Raw Diet, Medifast, Master Cleanse, soy, flaxseed oil, magic powders, creepy injections, sickening shakes, and then of course, there's always STARVATION. So many incredibly bad choices, and zillions of women (myself definitely included) can admit to doing some of the above at some point during our thigh-hating existence! It's a given: if a diet promises to smooth our tummies and slim our gams, we'll try it—no matter how heinous the method.

But here's the thing: since women seem to develop eating disorders in the womb, we're *used to* the torture of insane diets. On the other hand, men—unless they're heavily into sports, or are good friends with Carson Kressley from *Queer Eye*—have very little experience with the extreme agony, humiliation, discomfort, and unbelievable distress that comes with restrictive eating in the name of shaving off some extra pounds of unsightly fat and losing at least one of our extra chins in ten days or fewer! For the most part, men (especially old, bored, married ones) couldn't really care less about staying fit, and actually start using their enormous drooping bellies as entertainment, treating anyone around to their highly repulsive "talking stomach" performances.

So here's the plan, ma'am. You decide (in the name of overall health) to put your husband on a diet, and make sure you announce your brilliant plan just as he's reaching for the cheese puffs and the chocolate-dipped Double Stuf Oreo cookies. He might actually concede to your diet challenge, deciding it's high time to stop stuffing his pie hole with processed crap.

But what he doesn't know is that you've chosen the latest celebrity reduce-yourself-to-a-stick-figure regimen, and once he finds out what he's in for he'll be *begging* you to subject him to the barbaric tortures of waterboarding instead! Here are the top three most laughable, asinine, and severely questionable diets you might want to consider for your hubby:

- **Facial Analysis:** Some quack studies your face for markings, texture, and tone to discover your personal "mineral deficiencies." Then you receive a special diet plan to target your unique shortcomings to help you arrive at your ideal weight.
- **The Hallelujah Diet:** Somehow I doubt you'll be yelling out "hallelujah!" when you are busy taking hormone injections, undergoing colonics, and barely eating anything but shrubbery. Apparently, the diet gets its name because many "survivors" have claimed they've had spiritual awakenings while cleansing. (In my world these are called "hallucinations" caused by severe starvation.)
- **The Blood Group Plan:** The so-called "doctor" who came up with this diet seriously believes different blood types require different foods to help the body function at its fullest potential. "O types" are lucky. They get to eat lots of fat! Hooray!

31 Assault Him with Allergens

One of my coworkers (who requested to remain nameless because she pulls this con on a regular basis) is the source for this specific way of torturing one's mate.

Her hubby has suffered from severe, sometimes debilitating allergies from the time he was a child, and his condition only seems to worsen with age. It turns out pet dander is the main offender for my friend's husband, and as a result they have never had pets.

RISK INDICATOR: 4
Watch Your Back
Whatever you do, don't get busted being the dust fairy or get caught letting the dog sleep on your husband's pillow. You'll really be in the doghouse then!

This, however, hasn't stopped my coworker from having pets "visit" on occasion, and whenever the situation presents itself, she offers to pet-sit while her family members and close friends enjoy lengthy vacations, or overnight stays. Why does she do it? Because she knows it drives her husband crazy, and that's all she needs. When he complains (as well he should) she just shrugs it off by saying she "had no choice but to help out," then reminds him to take his medicine and avoid contact with the pet (even after the pet has contaminated the entire house during its stay.) I had a boyfriend who was allergic to dust. Whenever he pissed me off, I would invite him over and give my place a major dusting right before his arrival. The dust would inevitably trigger a range of symptoms (coughing, sneezing, watery eyes) and would sometimes result in an unpleasant asthma attack too! (Don't worry . . . he never left home without his inhaler.)

According to the National Center for Health Statistics, more than 26 million Americans suffer from hay fever or chronic seasonal allergies from blooming plants, grass, and pollen in the air, so if your man happens to be one of these folks, you can be a bit devious and bring some nature indoors, placing some offending flowers where your hubby won't see them, but definitely feel them when his allergies go into overdrive. You might also consider rolling in some freshly cut grass and then lying on his side of the bed, or opening all the windows on a warm spring day and just letting pollen land wherever it may. Milk allergies are apparently very prevalent as well (and milk is a substance that's pretty easily disguised in food!). But here's something to keep in mind: a milk allergy can cause immediate wheezing, vomiting, and hives, while being lactose intolerant will cause symptoms such as bloating, cramping, gas, and diarrhea. Both unpleasant, but very different. Speaking of unpleasant, a gluten allergy is pretty rare, but it does exist, and will definitely cause major stomach upset when offending carb quantities are ingested (just a spoonful of sugar might be enough!). Now let's be clear on this: While it may be fiendishly cruel to toy with someone's allergies and cause discomfort on purpose, this type of punishment should only be reserved for extreme situations, and you must take the solemn allergy pledge to never ever ever never ever (under penalty of girl-club eviction) go too far, or do this regularly. Anaphylactic shock is no joke, so remember, you've been warned.

According to the Centers for Disease Control, allergies are the sixth-leading cause of chronic illness in the U.S., with an annual cost in excess of $18 billion. More than 50 million Americans suffer from allergies each year.

32 Treat Him to a Treacherous Workout

I don't exercise. If God wanted me to bend over, he'd have put diamonds on the floor.
—COMEDIAN JOAN RIVERS

RISK INDICATOR: 2
Caution, Girlfriend
Make sure he doesn't overdo it! If he pulls a friggin' hamstring during one of these strenuous workouts you'll have to nurse the idiot back to health, and put up with his nonstop whining.

I remember when I was insane enough to sign up for a Power Yoga class with my girlfriend Patty. It was after enjoying a blissful, no-kids-around Saturday morning gossip-fest, while sipping venti, extra-shots, extra hot, Pumpkin Spice lattes at Starbucks. I was hyped on overpriced gourmet caffeine, and felt the need to do something wild and stimulating. Little did I know I would soon be begging for swift death once I found myself contorted in positions I couldn't imagine possible without the aid of Cirque du Soleil performers and a barrel full of Ben-Gay. Who needs this kind of pain to reach the path of enlightenment and relaxation? Silly me, I actually thought the "power" in "Power Yoga" meant "deeply spiritual," not "you need the strength of a BULL to get through it!" It turns out the form of yoga called Ashtanga is the preferred choice for athletes (definitely not me) and due to its physically demanding positions, is not considered suitable for beginners (undeniably me). I hid my tears during the downward dog, and avoided Patty's calls for two days (not because I was angry; it hurt to lift the receiver).

There's a reason you generally don't see men engaging in these ludicrous exercise routines, and it's because they have more common sense about these things than we women do (sorry ladies, I have to give this one to the guys). Men realize to get fit, you need not stray from the basics. Go for a jog, lift some weights, eat healthily (for the most part), and get plenty of sleep (in front of the television). Simple yet effective—and you get to skip the visits to a chiropractor for weekly adjustments. There is something to be said, however, about the excitement of trying something new, which is what we'll be nudging our men to do as we lead them down the dark path to grueling workouts, featuring annoyingly perky adrenaline junkies searching for their next fix. The choices are seemingly endless, and the exercise gods seem to crank out new, ultra-challenging fitness trends before we can even get used to the old ones!

For high-level husband torture you could consider one or several of the following options: painful Pilates, sadistic Swiss ball, heart-pounding cardio kickboxing, rigorous uphill spinning, core conditioning, and ache-inducing abdominal strengthening. Oh, and I definitely don't want to leave this one out (cue deafening Latin music) the art of ZANY ZUMBA! (Or as my fake-and-baked, too-tanned, exceptionally excited Portuguese instructor calls it: "Zooooooooomba Baybeeeee!") If you haven't been on the thrill ride called Zumba, you haven't lived a full life, and you owe it to yourself to sway to the hypnotic dance beats and sweat your cellulite-laden tushy off during a marathon hour-and-a-half class! There is one thing for certain when it comes to Zoooooomba, though. Coordination is absolutely required, so if your hubby is especially limited in the dexterity department (as most men are) you will laugh uncontrollably watching your man try to keep up. Zumba definitely is zany, and just what the doctor (or personal trainer) ordered!

Whichever exercise you choose, be sure to bring along plenty of fluids, and a couple of ice packs for the girly-man you call your mate.

33 Tamper with His Products

This is the kind of amusement you can have anytime, and there's not much planning that needs to be put forth, which makes it very appealing. All you need is a small motive. No seething required. For example, maybe your husband irked you as soon as you woke up

> **RISK INDICATOR: 1**
> *You're in the Clear*
> What can you say? Sometimes wacky things just happen!

and you're in the mood for a little revenge, or maybe you just owe him one for being a horse's ass recently, or you just feel like screwing with his head. I encourage you to try one of these pranks and see what you can get away with.

Just for fun, I like to hide my hubby's stuff and make him think he's starting to lose it. The best part is that this works with small stuff!

Deodorant, for example, is one of those items that seems to stay put; there's no plausible reason for it to disappear, so when it does it can be very frustrating. Swipe it from his medicine cabinet when he's not around and place it somewhere peculiar, like the refrigerator. You wouldn't believe how long that Speed Stick went undetected on the second shelf! My hubby was going nuts trying to find it all over the house. He kept saying, "Deodorant doesn't just get up and walk away! Where the hell could it be?" He questioned everyone, checked the garbage, looked under the beds, and rifled through the medicine cabinet several hundred times before he gave up and just bought another one, while I laughed myself silly. As I mentioned, you can do this with just about anything, and when you "magically" make the missing item reappear, and he'll seriously think he's delusional.

Other fun ideas for messing with your husband's stuff:

- Empty his cologne bottles, or his hair products, slowly over time.
- Replace the bulb in his night-table lamp with one that has less wattage.
- Pour cooking oil into his dandruff shampoo.
- Hide his watch or wedding band.
- Replace his protein powder with chocolate Quik.
- Extra-starch his shirts.
- Bend his eyeglasses or loosen the screws.

He'll have no explanation for what's going on, and he'll just have to file it under "unsolved mysteries."

34 *Wage War with the Thermostat*

Temperature control is a huge issue everywhere you go. Who hasn't sat in a restaurant complaining it's either "hot as hell in here," or "friggin' freezing"? You head to the theater at the height of summer and you need to bring a sweater;

RISK INDICATOR: 1
You're in the Clear
All is fair in love and temperature regulating.

go watch a sporting event and you're forced to make a paper fan out of your super-sized drink cup. It's a miracle we ever venture outside our homes and brave the drastic climate changes of the urban jungle.

As those who have the utmost pleasure of office employment know, workplaces also are a common battleground for hostile thermostat confrontations, forcing management to affix sturdy plastic lock-boxes over outlets in order to keep the peace. No one is safe from the fierce fight for temperature domination, although I've heard cease-fires do sometimes occur. But there *is* a place where the war never dies, where the struggle is constant and unbearable, and where man and woman are pitted against each other so viciously it'll send shivers down your spine.

That place is the average American home.

Have you ever seen a couple that agrees on a comfortable temperature? On average, it seems women are always cold and men are always hot, or vice versa when we're talking about a menopausal woman going through the "change." She brings it down to below freezing; minutes later he cranks it up to roasting. Studies should be done to see how much time we waste each day going to and from the thermostat looking to regulate our body temperature. Eventually the daily bickering turns to battle, kids choose sides, and things really start to get ugly. (Frankly, I'm surprised thermostats aren't mentioned more often in divorce proceedings. "Your Honor, I had chronic pneumonia and lost three toes to frostbite while I was married to that cold-blooded monster! I love him, but I just can't sleep in my coat anymore. I want out.")

Well, here is a great strategy to win the war once and for all. The next time you get your AC serviced, ask your technician to install one of those nifty thermostat covers on your unit, and hide the key! She who holds the key holds wins the war. But here's the catch: don't get a clear cover like they have at the office. A solid metal box is your best bet because your man won't be able to see what setting it's on. Another strategy you can use is the "cold feet attack," which is a nightly occurrence at my house. I patiently wait till my darling slips into bed, gets nice and cozy, and starts flipping through TV channels. That's when I pounce on him, pressing my cold feet on his back, thighs, or legs. He screams in agony and I laugh as he shudders. No matter how many times I've done this, he never sees it coming. When he complains that my feet are too cold, I tell him "That's what happens when you make me live like a penguin." Touché.

PROOF POSITIVE

Research shows that cold conditions at the workplace can actually reduce employee productivity, aggravate chronic health problems such as arthritis, and send energy costs through the roof. So don't be surprised if you're suddenly warmer than toast at work, and chickens start hatching.

35 Serve Him a "Special" Beverage

Water, water nice and cold
Who'd suspect
You come from the toilet bowl?
With bacteria you must be infested
By my hubby you'll be ingested
I will laugh
I am so clever
With my secret, sly endeavor
Here it comes
Just drink it down
Make sure nothing's floating 'round
Here's a toast to you, honey
The sewer line gave you your bubbly

> **RISK INDICATOR: 1**
> **You're in the Clear**
> Unless you actually open your mouth and spill the beans, your secret is absolutely safe! You might be tempted to tell him about your twisted game right after he's taken his final gulp, but I suggest you keep this one between you and the porcelain gods.

I know. Emily Dickinson never wrote profound prose about serving her husband toilet water. But then again, she wrote about funerals in her brain, spiders holding silver balls, and liquors she never tasted, so I wouldn't exactly call her normal! Plus, she never got married. If she had taken the vows, her poetry could have turned out even *more* dark and depressing! So let's discuss the merits of toilet water.

1. It is readily available. You don't have to go too far to find a finely equipped bowl amass with H2O.
2. Cats and dogs don't seem to mind quenching their thirst with clear refreshing water from the porcelain receptacle, and I've never heard of "toilet water poisoning," so how bad can it be?

3. I can guarantee that your husband's mouth has definitely been in (and around) other unsanitary places before, so you should feel just fine with this rather unconventional means of torture.

As for execution, I do believe serving toilet water "on ice" is probably the best way to go. Ice just gives it a more authentic just-came-from-the-fridge look so you'll be more apt to get away with it. I also believe you must act as natural as possible. Don't make a big deal out of it at all. Instead of offering him some water, which might arouse suspicion 'cause we all know we're not that nice, wait until your hubby works up a really dry mouth while doing some outdoor work, watching TV, or whatever he does to keep himself busy, and then follow through with the plan. Once he makes the specific request for water, casually fetch him a nice tall glass of "H_2O à la toilet." I'm sure you're sitting there considering this right now, and you're wondering how exactly you reach into the toilet without getting your hands wet during the process? Well ladies, sometimes torture requires a bit of discomfort, but when it comes to fetching the *agua*, just be swift and matter-of-fact. Gloves are a bit obvious, so the faster you can scoop up the water, the better. Using the actual serving glass is the best way to go. (A clear glass wouldn't be my first choice—too risky!) Fill the glass about three-quarters of the way up, wipe off any excess drops with some toilet paper, wash your hands, drop in some ice cubes, and serve with a smile! If your toilet water happens to be blue because of some silly sanitizer, skip the exercise entirely!

PROOF POSITIVE

From abcnews.com: "Fast-Food Ice Dirtier than Toilet Water" (February 20, 2006).

Jasmine Roberts never expected her award-winning middle school science project to get so much attention. But the project produced some disturbing results: 70 percent of the time, ice from fast food restaurants was dirtier than toilet water. The twelve-year-old collected ice samples from five restaurants in South Florida—from both self-serve machines inside the restaurant and from drive-thru windows. She then collected toilet water samples from the same restaurants and tested them at the University of South Florida for bacteria. In several cases, the ice tested positive for *E. coli* bacteria, which comes from human waste and has been linked to several illness outbreaks across the country. "These [bacteria] don't belong there," said Dr. David Katz, medical contributor to *Good Morning America*. "It's not cause for panic, although it is alarming because what she found is nothing new. You're not more likely to get sick now. But she's done us a favor by sounding the alarm." Both Roberts and Katz said that the ice is likely dirtier because machines aren't cleaned and people use unwashed hands to scoop ice. Toilet water is also surprisingly bacteria-free, because it comes from sanitized city water supplies. (Well water is another story. . . .)

36 *Stink Him Out with Perfume*

I recently had an odd yet enlightening conversation with my friend Ed. We were talking about the silly reasons people break up, and here's how it went down:

RISK INDICATOR: 4
Watch Your Back

Although his nose will never know you pulled this prank on purpose, you will be none too pleased if he starts wearing some revolting aftershave in the name of retribution.

Ed: I broke up with this girl even though I really liked her a lot.

Me: So you liked her, but you still got rid of her? That doesn't make sense.

Ed: Well, there was this one thing.

Me: Yeah, I figured there had to be something. So what was it? Did she have an extra toe, or "man hands," or something?

Ed: (Laughing) Oh gosh, no. It was her perfume.

Me: What do you mean, her perfume?

Ed: She wore this awful musky vanilla stuff all the time and it made me nauseous.

Me: So why didn't you just tell her that?

Ed: I did, but she refused to stop wearing it, so I dumped her.

Who knew a fragrance could be so powerful? It seems that just as a scent can be overwhelmingly pleasing, it can also have the exact *opposite* effect. What's fascinating to me is how Ed's girlfriend obviously enjoyed the bouquet of her perfume, but he was repulsed by it. This drastic contrast led to a drastic choice. (Ed now lives with a nice gal who smells much better.)

It is endlessly fascinating to me how our brain-scent connection can have such an impact, even on our decision-making, including what foods we'll eat, what products we'll purchase, which people we'll hang out with. A particular scent can also make your mind vividly conjure up memories, suddenly transporting you back to your mother's kitchen remembering the taste and smell of her just-baked banana bread. Take a whiff of rubbing alcohol, for example, and see where your brain takes you. Do you suddenly feel queasy, as thoughts of doctor's offices and needles flow through your mind? Scent is one heck of a sense, and it can definitely be used against you when you least expect it.

You should know your mate well enough by now to also know what kind of perfume drives him wild (in a good way), and what kind will send him running for the hills. Is he into musky, fruity, floral, woody, citrusy, spicy, or fresh oceanic fragrances? Maybe he's a naturalist, and prefers you to wear no fragrance at all. That's even better!

Drop by your favorite retail establishment and pick up the most assaulting, nostril- defiling, stomachache-inducing, highly concentrated perfume, eau de toilette body spray, mist, or splash you can get your hands on and declare it your new personal fragrance. Then proceed to bathe in it daily, pausing for reapplications should its potency wear off. Really douse yourself in it, your hair, your clothes, your bed, his car.

It won't take long before he complains of migraines and sleep disturbances. He might even suggest a new perfume for you to try that doesn't smell like mosquito repellent.

Sooner or later he'll be pleading for sweet relief.

PROOF POSITIVE

Did you know that as you age, you can actually lose your sense of smell? Health experts say our "smell years" peak in our late twenties or early thirties and gradually decline after that. The condition is called "anosmia," and is believed to be caused by viruses that attack the nasal cavity. According to the Anosmia Foundation, the true incidence of the condition is difficult to determine, although the National Institutes of Health has estimated that more than two million people in the United States suffer from some type of smell dysfunction.

37 Take Bondage to a Whole New Level

Some of you may already be familiar with the bondage scenario (you silly little freaks!) but many others have never traveled to this unfamiliar land, and wonder what dark and twisted encounters may lie ahead.

> **RISK INDICATOR: 5**
> *Run Like Hell*
> A little pain never killed anybody. In fact, pleasure and pain go hand in hand when we're talking S & M.

Fret not, my friend, bondage should cause you neither anxiety nor concern.

Actually, marriage is very much like bondage—it's a "bond" that definitely makes you "age," so you see, there's nothing to get excited about here . . .

Listen, the practice of sadomasochism (a fancy word for bondage) has been around for centuries, and in essence, the fetish world is mostly about using your imagination to break out of the norm and experience the fantasy side of sex.

Since our society generally frowns on radical behavior, many believe folks who enjoy sadomasochism are deviant and disturbed, but the truth is it's a common thread among all genders, races, orientations, and socioeconomic classes. According to *Psychology Today*, fantasies of sexual submission are widespread among women, even more so than among men. But how does this apply to your everyday life, and how can you use it to torture your man (in a way he won't necessarily enjoy)?

It doesn't take much to convince a man to take a walk on the wild side. Even the most conservative, tightly wound chap can't help but be enticed by the lure of kinky merriment! So here's the plan. Get your man incredibly excited as you explain the hot scenarios you would like to explore in the privacy of your boudoir. Break out the leather bullwhip (my favorite) and start slow and playful; blindfold him and lovingly tease him with some hot wax . . . But if you want to inflict some serious torture, go for the "Maria Special": Get your guy to let his guard down by offering a relaxing yet tantalizing sensual massage. Once he's naked, greased up, and sufficiently vulnerable, tell him it would really make your day to tie him up and ravish his staggeringly sexy body. He'll think he's in for an experience of a lifetime. And he is . . . only he'll surely want to forget about it when you get done with him! Use several of his own ties to strap him to the bedpost (or you can improvise and bind him to another piece of heavy furniture). Once he's tied up and secure, tell him you forgot the lubricant and just need to run to the store for a minute. He might protest, but he'll quickly see there's no point in arguing since he's bound like a wild circus beast. Make your exit, and take your time doing whatever you'd like. Run some errands, get a manicure. Stay out long enough to make him sweat, but return soon enough to evade felony charges.

Chapter Three

QUICK
TORTURE

38 *Pretend to Have a Secret Admirer*

I have a girlfriend who does this regularly and her husband always reacts accordingly; he goes off in a major huff. (Of course it never occurs to him to send his own wife flowers on occasion just to brighten her day, but dark is the day when his darling bride receives blossoms from some anonymous chap trying to woo her away!)

> **RISK INDICATOR: 3**
> *He Might Be On to You*
> There's a chance he might be jealous enough to go "007" and do some investigative work, possibly discovering your deception. Cover your tracks like a true pro.

Flowers are a funny thing, aren't they? They always look so marvelous, but eventually they turn to wrinkled masses of yuckiness that smell wretched and make you want to heave! Why is that anyhow? Why did Mother Nature construct something so lovely and enchanting that features a captivating aroma on one side, and an eventual repulsive odor on the other? We completely gush when presented with fantastic flowers, but the instant the beautiful bouquet sheds its final petal we unceremoniously cast it out with the rubbish!

Regardless of the end result, one thing is for sure: women definitely get a kick out of receiving them. Handpicked blooms are always welcomed, but I think most of us prefer the amusing arrangements that arrive via delivery. Indeed, women LOVE getting flowers—especially when they come from a "secret admirer." It makes us feel special, and for that reason it will make your husband extremely jealous!

Surprise Bouquet Execution: I know this might seem obvious, but here's an important reminder: DO NOT USE YOUR CREDIT CARD BECAUSE YOU WILL GIVE YOURSELF AWAY. For the "flower power" plan to go down smoothly, you must pay a personal visit to a florist, preferably not in your immediate area, AND PAY IN CASH so there is no traceable evidence. Once you've done the adequate browsing, pick the loveliest bouquet you'd like to bring home. As far as the note, don't get crazy and write too much or you'll give it away! Keep it brief, but be romantic enough to ignite his territorial male instinct and set him ablaze. Here's an example:

"Emily, you don't know me, but your beauty inspires me.
Thinking of you.
Your Secret Admirer."

Isn't that just perfect? Keeping it simple is the key to feeding your hubby's imagination. Your husband definitely knows that the way to a woman's heart is flowers and fine jewelry, so he'll be rightfully concerned about your "so-called secret admirer" and do his share of pouting and complaining. Don't be shocked if your husband asks you to throw out the flowers and the card once he find out about your "secret suitor." These items make him feel threatened, and men hate being upstaged. If he's smart you'll have an even bigger and more beautiful bouquet on your desk by Monday morning!

39 *Cause a Scene*

Never forget that despite all of our societal advancements, when it comes to men, they'd like to believe this is still the Wild Wild West, and they are the macho cowboys in charge. As you know, cowboys never lose control of anything—especially their women.

RISK INDICATOR: 5
Run Like Hell

You should try playin' 'possum (acting dead) when your man finally comes home (*if* he comes home, that is!), 'cause he'll want to wring your neck like a chicken if he gets ahold of you, girlie!

The truth is, men just don't like to air their dirty laundry, so they would do anything to avoid being publicly embarrassed in any way, or confronted out in the open where people can see and hear what's going on. The whole thing is extremely emasculating, which is exactly why doing it is so amusing.

There are many different ways to approach this. For example, the next time you and your husband are out at dinner, throw back a couple extra glasses of wine and pick a fight about absolutely anything. You know men are dim and can easily be lured into an argument, so it could be something as simple as "Honey, why haven't you told me I look nice tonight?" He'll probably respond defensively, and you can take it from there.

When you start getting loud and irrational he'll ask you to calm down, and that's when you turn on the waterworks and really start getting some attention. When he reaches out to you, give the ol' "Don't touch me" line, and storm out of the restaurant in a huff. He'll be so shocked he'll probably forget to pay the bill!

Another great way of causing a scene and embarrassing your man is to act inappropriately in front of his friends. Call your husband by his pet name and maybe pat his butt one too many times. Tell raunchy jokes, smoke a "stogie" if you have one, and act like one of the boys. Outrageous behavior will definitely get you some quizzical looks and angry stares.

For some real fireworks, crash your husband's next "Guys' Night" outing. That should be enough to turn him purple, but don't let it end there. Take it to the extreme by bringing your rowdiest girlfriends along. Once you arrive on the scene, steal the show. Make it your mission to drink too much, do a substantial amount of flirting, and get so boisterous your man will have no choice but to take you home or risk utter humiliation. Wouldn't it really be a hoot if his friends got such a kick out of you, they invite you along to every guys' night after that?

Oh well, your husband will have to find new friends.

40 *Delete His DVR Recordings*

I admit I pull this stunt VERY often and it always brings a gigantic smile to my face, as I'm sure it will to yours. You'll be smiling when you just think about doing it. The smile sticks around when you are actually doing the deed, and definitely lingers for a lengthy period

RISK INDICATOR: 3
He Might Be On to You

You can do this from time to time, but don't give yourself away by always deleting *Monday Night Football*. You'd become suspicious too, if your reruns of *Sex and the City* were constantly disappearing!

afterward. Laughter is also appropriate. For me there is a sense of thrill associated with DVR tinkering.

It has already been amply established that men can't get enough face time with their TV sets. They have become a man's electronic best friend/mate/significant other/babysitter/lover/therapist. The rapid spread of digital video recorders (DVRs) has only magnified this massive affection for the boob tube, creating a deeper bond and bordering on worship. (My husband adores this machine—he even dusts it from time to time!) TiVo has dramatically changed our lives. Now you can even program your DVR "on the go" from just about anywhere! At work, in the car, from the beach, maybe even from the surface of the moon!

But I have to ask: Is this *truly* necessary? Are you really going to drop dead if you miss the latest *American Idol* installment? Well, don't ask my husband that question. He unleashes a tirade under our roof when the DVR fails to record a scheduled event, "because one of your silly chick shows created a conflict!" My husband actually sides with the DVR because "it doesn't know any better, and just does what it's told!" That's when I start to hate that stupid thing. But it does have a special place in my heart, allowing me to enjoy primetime programming during my downtime hours when everyone is either out of the house or sleeping soundly in their cozy beds.

Those downtime hours also provide the ideal opportunity to discard his DVR recordings! He won't see you do it, so you can't be blamed! I don't recommend deleting ALL of his recordings, since this will obviously incriminate you. Instead, do a general scroll to find his most desirable recordings and get rid of those. Maybe he's mentioned something specific lately? Well, all you have to do is highlight it, delete it, and IT'S GONE IN A BLINK! That's when I kiss the remote and laugh my butt off!!

When he complains, you can always claim, "I have no idea what's gotten into that thing," or say something like "Ya know, we did have that power outage the other night. Oh gosh, I feel so sorry for you, sweetie. But don't worry, I'm sure they'll replay the *entire* Super Bowl sometime soon."

41 *Torch His Gorgeous Grill*

There's something about roasting animal carcasses outdoors that turns husbands into grunting, drooling, chest-pounding cavemen. Don't ask me what it is (because we all know the extent of their manly hunt was a trip to Costco for mammoth food portions and a stop for propane), but God knows men truly believe they are "testosterone titans" when they are manning that grill, decked out in a hat (or apron) and holding a big stick. Men just like the idea of calling the shots behind a desk, a wheel, a counter, or a shiny new Weber grill.

RISK INDICATOR: 2
Caution, Girlfriend
This joke is one that gets better every time you do it. He'll go from being mildly annoyed the first time to a swearing, sweating fool the third or fourth. Once he figures out you're behind the antics, run for cover.

One of the absolute worst offenders when it comes to boorish grillmeister behavior is my buddy Mitch, who's a gourmet chef. He goes from being your average shy, guy-next-door type (who knows his way around a kitchen) to Iron Chef Jackass when he gets behind the open flame of an outdoor cooking apparatus. Knives start flying, demands are barked with authority, and sweat pours from his wrinkled brow like the sizzling fat from a slab of choice prime rib. This is extreme grilling at its best.

Civilians gather to watch the flame-charring spectacle, but they know approaching the madman carries severe consequences. The grill god is at work. He should never be disturbed. Afterward, when the flames have subsided and the boisterous crowds have satisfied their hunger, you hear the calming sounds of a mighty grid brush in the distance being used with utmost care. The crunching and scraping bringing him closer to restoring the brilliant shine he treasures so much.

The grillmeister would rather eat sawdust than leave filth on his pride and joy. He will carefully remove every fraction of charred fat and tendons off his precious grill or die trying! He will not turn from this battle. Grill victory is at hand!

Wow, this is really going to be fun and oh-so-simple. Here's the plan to end his "Flintstonian" delusions. Most men will agree that when their mouth is watering for a tasty steak, the most annoying thing about grilling is finding an empty propane tank or running out of charcoal. If you know your hubby is planning on a night of grilling, and you have a propane tank, swap the full tank with an empty one. If it's a charcoal grill, empty the bag and hide the charcoal. Sit back and watch him piss and moan all the way to the store to refill the tank or pick up another bag of coals. If you do this every time he wants to grill, you'll have one angry husband on your hands.

42 Ambush Him in the Shower

There's a good reason that shower scene in *Psycho* was so deeply disturbing.

RISK INDICATOR: 2
Caution, Girlfriend
You can set him off in a vengeful tirade of attacks, and eventually nobody in your house will be showering, which can lead to an unpleasant-smelling situation.

Think about it. The shower is the one place where you not only want privacy, you expect privacy in every way. You're in there *naked*, for Pete's sake, as vulnerable and defenseless as the day you were ushered into this world! Your eyes are closed half the time as you enjoy the rush of warm water cascading down your head, face, shoulders, stomach, and nether regions. You may even try to sing that new song you love, but don't know the words to yet.

Anyhow, there you are, enjoying some blissful shower solace . . . easy prey for an intruder who wishes to disrupt this calming scene. You never see it coming, and that's why it's so disturbing. I'm still nursing deep psychological damage caused by my former college roommates, who carried out sinister shower attacks on our dorm floor. Not a day could go by without one of us suffering the "ice-water ambush" or the "pull the curtain back and take a picture" trick.

Your husband will soon share in your shower distress when he falls victim to your attack. You can start simple by stealing his towel or robe and work your way up slowly, or go for the full-on ambush: turn out the lights and pour freezing water over his head while yelling, "DEATH TO THE INFIDEL!" The flashbacks will haunt him for a lifetime.

43 Plan an Impromptu Kiddie Playdate

Does your husband get a case of the "crazy eyes" when he's suddenly thrust into something he didn't plan? My husband thrives on predictability, so any major (or minor) change in his schedule sends him into a panic, and he loses all control. It's like a vicious attack

> **RISK INDICATOR: 1**
> *You're in the Clear*
> If forcing him to spend quality time with his kids is a crime, call me guilty!

on his central nervous system; he gets huffy, confused, and downright angry. If you address his behavior, he'll become completely defensive, and blame you for being so inconsiderate and throwing him into the fire. But life with kids is like living in California. One minute you are happily skipping down Santa Monica Boulevard; the next minute an earthquake rocks your world and you find yourself huddled under an overpass wondering what the hell just happened. You have to expect the unexpected and just roll with it—or be washed away in the riptide!

In any event, the impromptu kiddie playdate is an ideal form of torture because there is nothing men love more than being pushed around by their wives and coerced into an unplanned activity involving your child and several other loud screaming rugrats, as well as their obnoxious parents. Hell, they should be able to handle it . . . we do it all the time! Women can do the playdate thing with their eyes closed, driving backward, texting a friend, and sipping a Diet Coke at the same time. How many times have you run into a girlfriend at the grocery store, decide to get the kids together, meet at a park thirty minutes later (with kids, snacks, drinks, and toys on hand), let them play for hours, and still get home in time to put a warm, healthy meal on the table before anyone even has a chance to ask, "Hey, what's for dinner?" That's just how efficient women are. Men, on the other hand, require a seventy-two-hour advance warning memo detailing the proposed playdate guests and suggested activities. If they actually agree to go on the planned outing, you have to pack the snacks, find the toys, and call your clueless husband eighteen times to make sure he hasn't lost one of the children or left one behind at Chuck E. Cheese.

The only thing worse than sending your husband on a kiddie playdate is making him go to a kid's birthday party completely SOLO. That's when the crapola really hits the fan. My husband literally called me in tears wondering why I would do such a horrible thing to him. He was so overwhelmed with the kids, the moms, the noise, and the roller coaster of action he nearly had a breakdown.

The next time your kids want to go on a playdate or have a birthday party to attend, book dear ol' Dad, and make some plans of your own. Pulling the rug out from underneath him serves him right.

44 Go on a Deluxe Shopping Spree

Find some comfortable shoes and do some pregame stretching. Shopping heaven, here we come! This is not for wimps—there will be no window-shopping allowed. If you want it you get it, and that's the only way to do it right. So if you love the smell of freshly cleaned mall linoleum in the morning, you've arrived at the right kind of torture. And if your husband happens to be a penny-pinching tightwad, he will be in serious misery following this exhilarating experience. (Note: The deluxe shopping spree works best if it totally catches your man off-guard, so don't do this around your birthday or any holidays—just pick a random day when he least expects a massive credit-card ambush.) Now, I know what you're thinking: *What if I don't have disposable funds to burn?* Girl, that's why the retail gods created the in-store lines of credit and the ninety-day return policy! Most retailers realize most of us can't afford the stuff we buy, so they offer the chance to get what you want—as long as you open an account with their particular company. It's a win-win situation for both parties if you ask me, but of course, don't get in over your head, and do proceed with caution. Decide how much you can realistically spend, make sure it will be enough to drive your hus-

> **RISK INDICATOR: 3**
> **He Might Be on to You**
> If you don't plan on letting your husband know about your shopping extravaganza, intercepting the credit-card bill is an absolute "DO." Letting him spot the diamond-encrusted tiara you may have purchased during your shopping spree is a definite "DON'T."

band nuts, and then go! When you are ready to execute the plan, grab a girlfriend, head out to your favorite mall or high-end boutique and crown yourself "Shopping Queen" for the day. Remember, everything goes, ladies, so whether it's couture apparel, off-the-rack fashions, sensational shoes, or the hottest handbags, ignore those price tags and treat yourself to whatever brings you shopping joy. By the way, just because we call it a *deluxe* shopping spree does not necessarily mean you need to purchase a truckload of treasures. My most recent "surprise spree" featured just one spectacular item.

As I already mentioned, shopping sprees do not have to involve a million items and they don't have to put you in debt for life, either. Just shop where you can get the most for your husband's hard-earned money! Either way you get what you want. Don't let anything stand in your way—just think of the great stuff you can get at an outlet or clearance center! We all have our favorite shops, so onward, ladies! Remember to pace yourself and stay hydrated.

PROOF POSITIVE

According to a Harris Interactive survey of 1,796 people ages 25–55, 29 percent of people in a committed relationship admitted to lying to their partner about their spending habits. Women were slightly more likely than men to be dishonest; according to the 2005 survey, 33 percent of women had something to hide, as opposed to 26 percent of men.

45 Invite Friends Over for an Extended Stay

Fish and guests in three days are stale. —GREEK PROVERB

If there's anything you learn quickly once you get married it's that people will suddenly come out of the woodwork looking to stay with you whether you have a guest room or not. Most don't even care if you have a bed available, as long as you have

RISK INDICATOR: 5
Run Like Hell
You'd better keep the guests around forever, because your number is up the second they head home!

cable and running water. This especially rings true if you happen to live in a tourist-desirable city. We made our personal "houseguests from hell" discoveries while living in Manhattan. It seemed the very day we signed the lease to a one-bedroom apartment on the Upper East Side, we were also barraged by phone calls from friends and relatives who suddenly had the urge to reconnect (and conveniently have free room and board) in the Big Apple. Even the most considerate, well-behaved houseguest becomes a pest when you are sharing close quarters, and it's hard to forget how often we found ourselves squeezed into our charming rent-stabilized apartment turned claustrophobic chicken coop. It is also during those types of situations when you become acquainted with your patience level, and determine your tolerance for guests and their wide range of personalities and shenanigans. It turns out my husband can barely make it through forty-eight hours of guest invasion. Me? They could stay as long as they want . . .

provided they occasionally clean up after themselves, and do not sleep naked (I've had a few eye-opening experiences through the years).

Regardless of sharp personality differences, I think most couples just treasure their privacy, and it's tough when your time alone is trampled on by a houseguest who wears out his welcome.

During my houseguest adventures, I also noticed something interesting. If the company in question happens to be a friend or family member, the visit always seems much more pleasant, and it is much easier to overlook any problems. That's why you need to invite some of your most obnoxious pals or relatives for an extended stay at your castle in order to get under your husband's skin. Don't give him any warning, either. Casually mention the sticky situation maybe the day before you have to pick up your delightful guests at the airport. If your visitors happen to be a couple, be extra considerate and offer your bed for them to sleep on. Be sure to appoint your hubby as official tour guide and driver. Plan day-long excursions to check out popular tourist spots, and make dinner reservations at several pricey restaurants where you'll also be picking up the tab. And don't forget to think BIG. If a house full of wild, screaming children will disrupt your hubby's Zen zone, extend an invitation to your friends who have the giant mini-van and four kids—all under the age of six. Let them take over the entire house with toys and clutter while your husband's blood pressure reaches high-voltage levels. Hopefully he won't blow until the last guest has left the building.

46 *Get a Tattoo*

If you always wanted a tattoo, but your husband said it was trashy, knock yourself out and get inked no matter what he says! What's he gonna do? Divorce you over a tattoo? It's just body art. It is your body, and he'll just have to deal. Hell, you put up with him every day, so accepting a little permanent ink on your body is not asking a whole lot.

> **RISK INDICATOR: 2**
> *Caution, Girlfriend*
> You might tick your husband off by getting a tattoo without warning, but remember this is permanent, and tattoo removal isn't as easy as it sounds!

I got my eyebrows tattooed once and my husband hit the roof! I had barely survived a horrific waxing accident at the hands of a novice and lost every strand of eyebrow hair, turning me into a freakish eyebrow-free alien for weeks. This was not a good look for me, so when one of my girlfriends suggested I get a cosmetic tattoo to lift my misery, I immediately made an appointment with a licensed aesthetician to get the job done.

I was thoroughly pleased with the results. I looked like a normal human again, and stared at my new "designer eyebrows" the whole way home.

But once I got home I wish I never had. My husband took one look at me and couldn't even put words together to form a sentence. I kept saying, "calm down, it's a cosmetic tattoo," but he couldn't bring himself to look at me for days.

Could you imagine his reaction if I came home with some intricate body art adorning my ankle, hip, back, or arms? I'd have to call for oxygen. But the truth is, they can freak out all they want; once it's done, they can't do a darn thing about it. It's been at least five years since "eyebrow-gate," and my husband doesn't even remember they are there.

If he can get over it, your husband will too (after you cause him severe aggravation first).

Be courageous and get that "tat" whenever you are ready. If you really want to cause a ruckus, get a naughty tattoo, and inscribe yourself with "sexy momma" or "sex kitten"—either would surely make your husband's blood boil. Tattoo placement can also cause quite a commotion. Have your chosen art placed in a somewhat risqué area, which will make him insane when you show it off to all of your mutual friends (including the male ones).

From what I hear among tattoo aficionados, once you've been tattooed, it is not rare to get "hooked on ink" and return for more. If you happen to be seduced by the lure of an artist's needle, your man is in for a good dose of trouble.

47 Stand Him Up on "Date Night"

Who came up with this ridiculous concept of dating your spouse? I thought the very reason we get married is to finally stop dating. To me, dating after marriage seems like drinking after rehab. (Then again, plenty of people do

> **RISK INDICATOR: 1**
> *You're in the Clear*
> Married dating is stupid anyway, so he had it coming.

that, so maybe I'm the nut case here.) Simple logical reasoning would tell you if you'd like to keep DATING, then why spend all that time, effort, and money getting MARRIED? Dating is clearly a less complicated, more cost-effective situation.

Yep, dating is for single people. The use of the word "dating" should cease entirely once you are married. In fact, your wedding rehearsal should officially be called your "Absolute Final Goodbye to Dating" date. You get decked out, you show up, and then the next day, or a couple days later: Ta da! Presto! You exchange vows, and never have to date again! How else are you supposed to know when to stop wearing makeup, throw out your razor, and stop pretending to enjoy his corny jokes?

It is all complete foolishness. Me? Dating? My husband? Absurd!

If I could go back to dating him I would dump him with a text message. But since we're married now, and we've bought into this whole idea of "date night" to keep our marriages remotely interesting, let's do something we would have done if our husbands had ticked us off while we were dating: Stand him up!

Of course you live together now, so it's a little more challenging than you think, but if you arrange to meet him right after work, your plan will come together just fine.

The goal is to let him get to the restaurant, the concert, or movie theater (pretty much the only places married people go), and just let him wait . . . and wait . . . and wait. He'll be positively peeved, and incredibly embarrassed by the fact that he was stood up by his own wife! Don't pick up the phone when he calls, or respond in any way.

He'll eventually decide to head home wondering if something terrible has happened to you. But he'll find you there, sleeping soundly in your cozy jammies. Just tell him you didn't feel well and you assumed he got your message (you know, the one you never sent!).

Promise to make it up to him, and go back to sleep with a smile.

48 *Mess with His Computer*

My husband has two speeds; grumpy and grumpier. In all fairness, I did enter into our idyllic union completely aware of this not-so-pleasant character flaw, but there's something about fussy electronics that sends him into hyper-overdrive grumpy mode, especially when they don't perform as expected.

His reaction is like watching a Jekyll and Hyde transformation, going from calm and controlled to possessed and homicidal. In case you're wondering, I am not being overly dramatic for effect; he admits he has an irrational short tem-

> **RISK INDICATOR: 1**
> *You're in the Clear*
> Computers are as fickle as hormonal teenagers. There's no way he can blame you for his computer woes unless he's got proof, so leave none behind. For your own benefit, stay away from important financial files (you don't want to mess with his credit cards; this could backfire bigtime)!

per for these things, and it turns out many men suffer from the same affliction. I think it's another one of those testosterone issues women will never understand. Control is the central factor here, and if there's anything a man should be able to control it's his home electronics! This is especially true when it comes to our home computer. God forbid it suffers a slight glitch or takes too long to perform an appointed task. My husband cries conspiracy, gravely convinced the hard drive is taunting him on purpose. If this sounds familiar, it's time to make your guy's conspiracy theory come true, and really send him through the roof.

If you ever hang out with tech geeks you'll soon discover they're very handy to have around because they have some wicked tricks for sabotaging a computer. Here are a just a few suggestions. By the way, you don't need a master's from MIT to pull off any of this:

- Hide, rearrange, disable, or delete icons and programs.
- Invert his right click and left click mouse functions on the computer control panel.
- Remove the batteries from his wireless mouse.
- Hide important files.
- Assign the computer a task so that every day at the exact time his computer will suddenly play Michael Bolton's greatest hits.
- Perma-block his favorite websites (especially espn.com).
- Change his access rights, banning him from installing new programs.
- Delete his entire iPod library (but back it up first!).
- Program an icon to automatically shut off his computer once he clicks on it.
- Hack into his saved PDA contacts and scramble a bunch of names.
- Disconnect his modem, fiddle with his wires, and make his hard drive look like a hot mess!

If for some reason you can't perform any of the above-mentioned duties, you can always find a computer-savvy accomplice to aid with the tampering. It might cost you a little bribe money, but it will be well spent when your husband spends hours trying to figure out why his PC suddenly has a mind of its own.

49 Toss His Stuff on the Lawn

Sometimes you just have to treat men like children. In reality they never grow up, yet somehow we marry them and expect them to act like adults (which is rather foolish on our part). Expecting a man to act like a grownup is like expecting your eight-year-old to pay taxes and stop making fart jokes.

> **RISK INDICATOR: 2**
> *Caution, Girlfriend*
> What if you came home and found your new Gucci bag on the lawn? I shudder to think . . .

There are many opportunities in a day to treat your man like a child:

- Put out his clothes for him, since he can't dress himself.
- Give him a time-out when he misbehaves (meaning ignore him completely when he acts like an insensitive jerk).
- Force him to eat his vegetables at dinnertime or no dessert.
- Remind him constantly to mind his manners.

But there's one rule I would say about 85 percent men break quite often, and no punishment ever seems fit. The rule is this: Don't leave your crap all over the floor. My new punishment is: Whatever I find on the floor, you will find on the lawn. This applies to every and all items. Clothing, shoes, books and magazines, electronics, silverware, beverages, plates, trash; men just seem to like the floor so much, it's rare to find something actually placed on an actual counter. But let your man know there's a new sheriff in town, and she means business.

Clothes are my husband's favorite items to just drop on the floor and walk away from. Pardon me, but was there some kind of rush? Are you a firefighter who needs to drop trou and run? For some reason, the discarded clothes issue really boils my hemoglobin. But he'll change his tune the second he comes home and finds his Calvins hanging from one of the bushes in the back yard. By all means, use the front yard too (especially if you don't mind the frightened stares from neighbors). Your man would learn his lesson right quick. Can you imagine coming home and finding all your possessions strewn about for everyone to see? Just think of the look on his face.

I got so mad once after tripping over one of my husband's stupid sneakers, I grabbed the pair and chucked it out the bedroom window. Hours later when my husband got home and was headed out to soccer practice with my son, he was going nuts looking everywhere for his sneaks. Finally he spotted them outside the window and ran out to rescue them. By then, an army of ants had moved in, and some clumpy bird poop was part of the exterior design.

I felt kind of bad because it turned out the sneakers were brand new, he had only worn them once, and had paid top dollar, but we haven't had any shoe incidents since then!

If men want to act like children, your only solution is to treat them as such. Set the rules and they will follow. Whether they like it or not.

50 *Invade His Office Space*

Ambushing your husband at work is a surefire way to send him into hysterics. In my opinion, men go to work to avoid dealing with their wives, so they'll be pretty unnerved if you suddenly show up and rock his world. Believe me, I've done this, and he absolutely hated it!

RISK INDICATOR: 4
Watch Your Back
You might be starting a war, and the backlash won't be pleasant.

But don't take it personally; on average, most men (at least the successful ones) are pretty private about their personal lives at work, and besides a few required family photos on their desks, they prefer to keep those two worlds from colliding. You'd be surprised to know how many wives I've spoken to who have *never* been to their husband's offices, and are just known as ghosts on the phone who occasionally speak to a receptionist or coworker.

Well, your ghost days are over, Missy. It's time to make your long-awaited office debut! Clear some time on your schedule when you know he'll be in the office, pick up an elegant muffin or cookie basket (to earn brownie points with the staff), and just drop by completely unannounced. Guys really freak when their wives become "office invaders." They get that shocked-anxious-perplexed-suddenly-want-to-vomit look, but they have to keep it together because all eyes are suddenly on them. It's an intoxicatingly awkward situation, and seeing your hubby sweat through it elevates it to another level. Once you show up, you'll be thrust onto center stage and your husband is forced to introduce you to all his nosy coworkers looking for fresh water-cooler gossip. (If your man happens to be The Boss, wifely visits are even MORE tension-inducing.) Be your graceful, charming self and become acquainted with his staff—while your husband fights every urge in his body to have you escorted from the building by security. If you've already been to his office, another exciting way to raise his blood pressure is to bring the kids by to say hello!

If your surprise visit isn't enough to give him a panic attack, this will no doubt do the trick. Staying extra long will just add to his day gone bad, so don't rush off; plan to stick around for lunch or a coffee break. If he's not available, be bold and invite his receptionist or assistant. It's always a good time to get the latest office gossip—or start some of your own. He'll really love that. Maybe if the office ladies like you enough they'll invite you to their next office happy hour! You never know what kind of information you might discover. Isn't your husband always complaining that his office is such a bore? Well, here's your chance to shake things up and provide some stimulating excitement.

51 *Sign Him Up for Oprah's Book Club*

Dear Oprah:

Ever since the my high-school days when my classmates voted me "Most Likely to Become the Next Oprah Winfrey," I've dreamt of the moment we would finally meet face-to-face when I'd immediately replace Gayle as your new BFF. Not only would you give me a free car and some stunning, ten-carat diamond earrings (because you are so incredibly generous), you'd also invite me and Maya Angelou for lunch at your lovely ranch in Indiana, where we would all share a decadent meal, spend countless hours reading poetry, and eventually discuss how you would be thrilled to have ME fill your billion-dollar shoes on *The Oprah Winfrey Show*!

> **RISK INDICATOR: 1**
> *You're in the Clear*
> Whether you deny involvement or tell the truth, it's a "no harm, no foul situation" all the way. However, if marital counseling is necessary, just dial 555-ASK-DR-PHIL.

That's my "Wildest Dream," Oprah. Let's make it happen.

Okay, so maybe I'll never meet Oprah (or even get to drive past her ranch in Indiana), but we can *all* get infinitesimally closer to her by taking one incredibly simple step. Join Oprah's Book Club.

Signing up for Oprah's Book Club, or in this case, signing up your unsuspecting man, isn't a simple matter, folks. No, Nee, Nyet, Na, Nun, Ngai, Nie. Not on your life! First you have to answer a lengthy list of probing personal questions including, "What's your birth year?" (as if that's anyone's beeswax), and whether or not you worship Dr. Phil (which was the toughest one for me, but heck, I'll lie in a New

York millisecond to get closer to Oprah!) Once you've made it past the hard-core questionnaire, prepare yourself for an overwhelming e-mail assault of sappy, motivational newsletters, countless webinar invites, and dull video lectures. Plus, your inbox will be filled with a relentless deluge of message board offerings that will make your head spin. It's a miracle your hard drive doesn't crash!

For this reason, you must make sure to offer your man's personal AND work e-mail addresses! Picture your husband sitting at his desk when he receives his "Oprah.com Membership Confirmation!" Wouldn't it be uproariously funny if one of his buddies happens to glance at the monitor? Painfully comical—and you can actually deny you had anything to do with it! *Anyone* could be the culprit. You can even blame scheming spammers for the deed. A computer is all you need to get the job done, and even if your hubby terminates his membership(s) immediately, it will be worth it just to see him cringe.

52 *Pull a Disappearing Act*

Looking for some peace and quiet? Desperate to spend some time alone without a husband or children hanging around? Well, here's your chance to do just that without an ounce of guilt, and with the added benefit of

RISK INDICATOR: 1
You're in the Clear
One is *not* the loneliest number after all! Everyone deserves to be alone for a while, so hatch your plan and get crackin'.

giving your husband a sizable dose of stress and panic. I do this so often my husband is already used to it, but it will work wonders for a first-timer. I guarantee it!

I know we get married for love and companionship, and we have kids to further solidify that loving bond and fulfill our need for family. The thing nobody tells you when you finally get married and have a family is how you will never have a moment to yourself ever again, and how you will treasure a simple solo drive to the dry cleaners just so you can have a few precious moments by yourself without interruption, pleas for food and attention, nonstop questions, and constant mental drainage—and that's just from your husband! The children bring it to an even higher level . . .

So this is what you do when you are ready to seize the day, and claim it entirely for yourself. If you are a working gal, schedule a personal day, or simply take a day off (and don't tell your husband about it because he'll just ruin your plan).

If you do the stay-home thing, just leave a day wide open so you can drop the kids at school and then VANISH. In order to avoid being placed on a Missing Persons list, make one phone call to your husband. Let him know only that you will be completely unreachable throughout the day, but you'll be fine and not to worry.

That whole maneuver is about strategy. By telling him everything is fine and not to worry, he will worry even more, and wonder what you are up to. He'll probably think you're busy packing up your bags and taking off, but you will just be enjoying one delightful day free of tedious wifely disturbances. You deserve it, dammit, so don't allow guilt to ruin your one special "ME" day. Put those thoughts aside, and take a ride on the "It's All about Me for a Change Express." Choo Choo!!

For this to really work, you must part with any electronics for the day. That means, whether you stay home and just relax or head out for a solo adventure, you can't answer your cell phone or home phone, no texting or online chatting, and you can't send or receive e-mail. Same goes for snail mail, fax, skywriting, messenger pigeon, and any other means of communication I somehow missed. Men get very disturbed and frustrated when they can't reach us, which just proves we're always too available for our own good!

Believe it or not, becoming a ghost for a day isn't as easy as it sounds. There are forces working against you, and your man will call urgently wanting to know what you're really up to and attempting to make you feel bad for wanting to just get away.

Frankly, it's none of his business and you can tell him that straight up, sistah! Fight hard to spend time getting to know yourself again. You'll thank yourself later on and drive your hubby crazy in the process.

53 *Get Rid of His Porn*

Here's a wake-up call, ladies. Listen closely and let this sink in ever so gently.

EVERY MAN (no matter how innocent, kind, educated, and seemingly normal he may appear) HAS HIS VERY OWN PRIVATE PORN COLLECTION THAT HE DESPERATELY CAN'T WAIT TO ENJOY WHEN NOBODY IS AROUND. That "collection" can be as vast as the ocean (featuring every single issue of *Hustler* magazine printed since its debut in 1974, as well as an impressive array of high-quality porn videos, and a plethora

Men are very protective of their porn (which they tend to bond with over time) so if you are aiming to get rid of it, don't drop any hints because he'll know you're on to him and he'll just move his collection to a new, "safe" location. You may want to wait till he's out of town to implement your plan.

of naughty specialty sex toys) or as limited as Pamela Anderson's IQ (consisting only of a couple of key *Playboy* issues, some torn-out pages from a Victoria's Secret catalog, and a dusty VHS version of *Debbie Does Dallas*). Men just can't get enough of porn, and it is a solid certainty your husband's stash is somewhere in his closet or dresser, under the bed, beneath the mattress, maybe even tucked discreetly under the bathroom sink, but I assure you he has one—and it is your job to find it. Pay attention to details. Is your man particularly protective of a certain file in his home office? Does he spend an inordinate amount of time in a certain part of the house? If so, that's probably where you can locate his stash! And don't even rule out the kitchen or garage; men get pretty darn creative when it comes to hiding their twisted porn stockpile. For all you know, he may even be keeping it in his car or on his computer! But if you've sniffed around and can't seem to zero in on your target, you can always set up an Amateur Porn-Surveillance System.

Make use of that camcorder gathering dust in the corner. Set it up in a discreet spot and let the camera be your eyes and ears! A man's gotta do what a man's gotta do, so women should follow suit to find the necessary evidence. Here are the three rules for dealing with a man's pornography compilation:

1. Don't wonder *if* your guy has a stockpile of porn . . . just wonder *where* it may be.
2. Once the obscene stash is discovered, move in swiftly. You never know when he'll be itching for a fix!
3. If confronted about his missing X-rated stash, confess nothing and quickly redirect his attention with food and beer.

54 Drink His Last Beer

I would kill everyone in this room for a drop of sweet beer.—HOMER SIMPSON

I believe there is a Homer Simpson living inside every man, although I know there are plenty of men who would forgo a frosty

> **RISK INDICATOR: 2**
> *Caution, Girlfriend*
> There is a reason they call them "beer bellies," ladies. Beer can be very fattening, so watch those calories and stick to the light versions whenever possible.

pint for a nice glass of wine, or pass on the booze altogether. Those guys have officially lost their "Man Cards" though, because we all know *real men* live to drink beer.

I had my first swig of beer when I was about nine years old. Don't freak out—it's not like my parents held a kiddie kegger. I actually swiped my dad's ice-cold Miller Draft when he wasn't looking, and he still has no idea how that beer just got up and walked away. The heist went down on a blazing-hot summer day. My dad was diligently mowing the lawn (and kicking back a six-pack) when he left a bottle unattended, and I moved in for the kill. I had to be swift. Getting caught was not an option. My hand trembled as I brought the frosty beverage to my lips. I knew this was it. I was finally going to find out what beer tasted like after years of being told it's for "adults only," and I would be able to drink it someday when I had kids my age. (Like I had that kind of patience!) The anticipation was driving me mad, so I took a giant gulp and almost choked on the frigid amber liquid. It was sweet yet bitter, bland yet strong. I wasn't sure if I liked it, so I took another swig . . .

Let the record show that my first taste of beer was the last for years to come. Later in high school, I did my share of sneaky underage drinking, then learned how to professionally handle a beer bong and funnel in college. (Practice makes perfect!)

These days I still like beer, but my tastes have changed. I now prefer mixed drinks like Cosmos and vodka-cranberries. Occasionally I have a beer, but only when it is the last one in the fridge because

I know my husband will flip his lid and cry like a lost four-year-old girl.

Everyone hates it when someone eats or drinks something that belonged to them. You feel violated and angry, which is *exactly* how your hubby will feel when you disregard his love of lager, crack open his last beer, and mercilessly chug it down. You can do it right in front of him (and enjoy every last chilly drop) or drink it when he's not around and let him find out on his own. Just think, he'll be desperately searching for his brew and instead will discover he's been "beer punk'd" by a girl.

55 *Put a Stop to His Snoring*

There are moments in life when you find yourself on the edge, and you realize you are mere moments away from drifting off to dreamland.

And then you hear it—thunderous guttural roaring coming from your husband's mouth. The same violent snoring you deal with every night, rousing you from your slumber just as you are about

> **RISK INDICATOR: 5**
> *Run Like Hell*
> If he has any energy left after everything you plan to put him through, sleeping in the guest room isn't such a bad idea after all!

to enter peaceful oblivion. It is at this point you weigh your options and begin the following internal dialogue: "Gosh that's loud. I wonder if the kids can hear it on the other side of the house? This is so unfair, everyone is resting but me. Look at him, mouth all hanging open, drool trail oozing from his bottom lip. He couldn't be happier right now. Should I nudge him lovingly and hopes he stops? Maybe shaking or pushing him slightly will force him to shift and change positions. I should just go sleep in the other room. Wait a minute, why should I be the one to leave? He's the one who's growling like a grizzly! Screw it, I'll just smother him with my body pillow." My heart goes out to every woman who deals with this on a nightly basis.

Some women say after years of sleepless nights you somehow get to a place where you don't even hear the snoring anymore. Maybe acceptance eventually kicks in, or maybe you just go deaf from the noise. Hell if I know, but I say if you're being tortured from lack of sleep, revenge should be yours.

Snoring doesn't just "go away." In my opinion it worsens with time, but there are plenty of "remedies" you can force your husband to try—or else. (He knows what that means, trust me. He doesn't want to be subjected to a midnight smothering.)

Phase 1: Start with the basics—sleep posture correction and anti-snore pillows. Since most people snore more loudly while sleeping on their backs, there are strap-on cushions available (shaped like a thick, square backpack) that make it uncomfortable for a snorer to roll onto his back, therefore reducing the snoring. As for anti-snore pillows, these are designed to align a snorer's head, reducing obstructed breathing during sleep. (They don't look too cozy.)

Phase 2: If posture correction or special snore pillows don't do the trick, advance to the use of Breathe Right nose strips. This is the most popular snoring remedy, consisting of a plastic adhesive band placed across the nose to widen the nasal valve and maintain constant airflow. Herbal remedies such as Z-Snore throat spray reduce inflammation of mucus membranes, aiding respiration. Or purchase some Chin-Up Strips, which are hilarious facial adhesive "bandages" that basically keep your mouth from drooping opening so you don't snore. If none of this works, move on to Phase 3.

Phase 3: Mouthpieces. These devices are mostly available from your dentist and prevent soft throat tissues from collapsing and obstructing the airway. Mouthpieces can be uncomfortable and expensive, and are abandoned by a high percentage of users.

Phase 4: CPAP (continuous positive airway pressure) is a popular obstructive sleep apnea treatment involving the use of a machine that increases air pressure in your throat, keeping your airway open. In severe circumstances surgery is sometimes performed, including a procedure called a *uvulopalatoplasty,* which removes or shrinks the palate and throat tissue, allowing air to flow.

Phase 5: Smother him with his strap-on anti-snore cushion. Hear that? It's called silence. Your job is done. Sweet dreams.

56 *Mess with His Favorite Ties*

I decided torturing my husband via his ties would be a fantastic form of revenge because he simply has too many (and he likes them a whole lot), buying them in all different parts of the world. I guess it's his nerdy pastime— one of the hazards of life in the corporate world, I suppose. Last I counted, his col-

RISK INDICATOR: 3
He Might Be On to You
Never start with his absolute favorites, and alternate between patterns and solids so as to not be detected.

lection was up to an absurd number, three hundred, far more than my shoe total, which is just unfair in my book. Actually my husband would have more ties if it weren't for the fact that I take it upon myself to "dispose" of them quietly. Since I can't put HIM through the shredder, I take my rage out on his collection. A little sick maybe, but let's not point fingers. Let's just stick to the "ties" that bond us (pardon the pun).

So what's the story with neckties anyway? I've spent some time pondering the purpose of a tie, and I couldn't come up with a good answer. Unlike suspenders, ties don't hold anything up, they aren't necessary like pants, and a man can obviously wear a shirt without one. Ironically, just like the men who wear them, it turns out ties are pretty useless. I do, however, believe the necktie has some merit and can be pretty cool in some ways (like yanking on them to get a man's attention, or using them in a bondage scenario).

A 2007 "tie" Gallup poll found that only 6 percent of American men wear neckties to work every day, down from 10 percent in 2002, but for those whose jobs still demand proper attire, ties are still a symbol of distinction (and a handy napkin should you need one in a pinch). However you screw with your husband's ties (hiding them over time, shredding or taking scissors to them, burning them), do it slowly and savor the moment. There is one of my husband's ties I wouldn't dream of touching, though. It's a special Calvin Klein black and gray tie that sits way back in his closet. He wore it on our wedding day, I picked it, and it's still the nicest one in the bunch.

57 Send Him on a Hellish Grocery Store Hunt

A kryptonite-like task men utterly despise is the obligatory trip to the grocery store (which needs to be done at least once a week, but somehow always seems to catch them by surprise: "You're going to the grocery store? AGAIN?"). Women usually tackle the grocery grunge work alone, leaving the men in our lives blissfully unaware of the

> **RISK INDICATOR: 1**
> *You're in the Clear*
> He might eventually figure out you sent him on a wild goose chase, but you'll have plenty of Karo Syrup to sweeten him up with.

myriad items available in that large building they naturally avoid. I swear on my meatloaf, the last time my husband joined me at our local supermarket, I heard him cheerfully exclaim, "No way, they actually give FREE SAMPLES at the deli?" Since they are so unfamiliar with Grocerystorelandia, mess with your man's head and send him off with a lengthy list of hard-to-find, perplexing, or simply nonexistent items.

Here's a sample list to illustrate:

Lavender mustard
Fresh tarragon
3 EXTRA LARGE kiwis (I'd *kill* to see him standing there dazed
  and confused)
2 grass-fed beef filets
Tahitian vanilla
Moulard duck breast
Liquid cilantro (basically impossible to locate)
Raw couscous
Smoked mutton
Karo Syrup (not too hard to find, but great with French toast)

He'll call after five minutes of searching, but since your cell phone will be turned off, he's SOL. You won't see him for hours, so take advantage of your newfound free time on Saturday afternoon!

58 Take Up an Annoying Hobby

I'm not much of a hobby person. Just the word "hobby" makes me cringe. It summons incredibly nauseating thoughts of scrapbooking and stamp-collecting. Who has time for this stuff? Quite frankly, if I had any spare time on

> **RISK INDICATOR: 1**
> *You're in the Clear*
> As long as you're smiling and he's cringing, it's all good in the hobby 'hood.

my hands, I'd rather do more of something called "absolutely nothing." I think more people should enjoy the simple pleasure of nothingness. But alas, nothingness proves to be somewhat of a challenge in this over-achieving society. We are so used to filling up every tiny moment of our time, we've become terrified of the mere idea of just being blissfully and unequivocally lazy. Actually, if "lazy" can be listed as a hobby, I guess I've been a hobby person all along and I didn't even know it!

As far as annoying your man by taking up a new hobby is concerned, you'll want to do a little research first. After all, you don't want to do something you're going to absolutely detest in the name of torturing him. You should choose something that might actually bring you some modicum of excitement or pleasure. I've actually always dreamt of playing the guitar, the electric guitar. That's just the kind of hobby that would get under my husband's skin. It's a wild, noisy, and in-your-face kind of annoying. That's exactly what the hobby doctor ordered because it would provide both pleasure for me and pain for him (in the form of eye-popping headaches).

Another hobby you might consider in the name of husband torturing is something intense and dangerous like . . . race-car driving. I know it sounds kind of nutty, but I have a friend who started doing this for kicks and she's totally hooked! Her husband hates it because:

a) It's definitely dangerous.
b) She's got a whole new set of race-car buddies who just HAPPEN to be men.

c) She looks devilishly hot in her ultra-sexy racing jumpsuit with matching heels! Apparently one of her friends gave her race-car driving school lessons as a gift, and it became much more than a simple hobby; it's now her all-consuming obsession—and her husband couldn't be more peeved. Other "sporting hobbies" that would surely annoy a hubby or send shivers down his spine include target shooting ('cause you learn to handle a gun), kickboxing ('cause you could kick his ass), and there's always fencing ('cause you could maim him for life). Okay, JUST KIDDING on that last one!

And finally, you can always take up an extraordinarily dull hobby like painting, photography, nature walking, or pottery (no offense to those who enjoy the duller side of hobbying) and try to get your hubby roped in along with you!

Whatever you pick, just make sure you get some kind of fun out of it. Well, then again, seeing the look on his face when you tell him you've taken up extreme freestyle skateboarding (and are planning to build a giant ramp in your back yard) will surely make it all worthwhile.

PROOF POSITIVE

According to Harris Interactive, the list of the most popular hobbies and leisure activities in descending order are as follows: TV watching (Really? This, a "hobby"?), spending time with family/kids, fishing, gardening, swimming, computer activities, movies, traveling, music, and shopping.

59 *Use His Picture for Target Practice*

Whether you invite some of your most fun-loving friends over, or just need to blow off some steam solo, you can't go wrong with this kind of entertainment! Who doesn't like to engage in some impromptu target practice? There's just something inside all of us that forces us to take a shot when walking past a dartboard, right?

RISK INDICATOR: 4
Watch Your Back
Keep in mind darts tend to be sharp and can be quite painful should they land in unwanted places.

You know it's true. You try your darnedest to casually stroll past that bull's-eye at the bar, but you can't resist; you have to throw at least one dart and see where it lands (hopefully not in someone's eye or drink). You know exactly what I'm talking about. It's like there's a highly competitive sportsman lying dormant inside all of us who is suddenly awakened at the sight of a dartboard. And isn't it great when that dart lands in the sweet spot? It's the closest feeling to unexpectedly winning the lottery, and you have to utter that necessary "YES-SSSSSssssss" to make sure everyone in the entire bar acknowledges your major achievement. You hit the bull's-eye, dammit, and you are as proud as a peacock. That's exactly the feeling we're going for here. Using your husband's picture for target practice will excite you in more ways than you ever thought possible. And talk about cheap entertainment! It's practically priceless, and definitely goes a long way.

So here's the plan, amigas. Get a flat piece of one-inch plywood for your backing (it doesn't matter if it's not round) and ask one of those cute boys at the store to drill a couple of holes at the top so you can hang it up. Buy some darts at any sporting goods store, and don't spend too much time there because we have more work to do. Next, find a particularly annoying picture of your husband in your digital picture library (maybe one where he looks all smug and full of himself, or just looks completely ridiculous because he's got bad hair or something in his teeth) print it out (8" × 10" will do just fine) and tape it or glue it onto the piece of wood. Then use a thick marker to make six concentric circles on the picture and assign corresponding number values. The average dartboard starts with the number 100 in the center circle, and then goes in descending order, 75, 50, 25, 10, and 5 for the outside circle. (I actually assign "shots" along with the numbers to really make the game interesting. Tequila works fine for me, but you can pick your own poison of course!) Believe me, after a couple of rounds you won't even remember why you were ticked off in the first place! You can also play for points or cash, and inviting your husband to join in the fun will definitely add to the torture element. But after a couple of shots, you'll both have a great time. If you can find a full-body pic of your nearest and dearest you're really in business 'cause there's nothing better than planting a dart directly on his "frank and beans!" You can also get creative by using fun stuff like eggs, paintballs, fruit, or whatever you can get your devious little hands on. Hey, how about getting the girls together for a "Hubby Target-Practice Party?" Get your game on . . . and aim low, girlfriends. Aim low.

60 Act Like a Teenager

No, I'm not talking about having a midlife crisis (although I guess you can technically call it that if you go from being a conservative housewife to local party girl).

I mean suddenly becoming a moody, mysterious, melodramatic (where did all these *m* words come from?) withdrawn, tortured soul who barely speaks, and when you do, it's only to utter over-the-top theatrical statements like, "No one understands me!"

RISK INDICATOR: 1
You're in the Clear
Some call it a midlife crisis; others call it getting in touch with your inner adolescent. Either way, you're entitled to act a little crazy on occasion, so don't let anyone stop you.

"I hate you!" "Why don't you just leave me alone?" "My life sucks." And the ever-popular "I'm not talking to you, I'm leaving!"

Gosh, I wish everyone could do this, because this is one of the techniques I tried not too long ago, and I honestly believe I have plenty of repressed teen angst still begging to be purged, despite the fact that my thirty-something body can't keep up! It turns out being a teenager isn't easy. All that tension and defiance can be very draining, especially when you couple it with staying up waaay too late texting your friends, eating tons of greasy fast food, and coming home at least five hours after curfew. So why do teenagers act this way? Just as in the "toddler phase," teens are testing your limits, separating from you, and looking to establish their own identities. If you happen to have a teenager under your roof, consider yourself ahead of the game. Many of us have to jog our memories to remember what it was like. Unfortunately, I was so terrified of my mother I walked a pretty straight line during my teen years. My mother swore to me (and I still believe her to this day) that, "as easily as I brought you into this world, I could just as easily take you out should you do anything stupid to embarrass me in public!"

As you can understand, with threats like those I was a pretty good kid, and the closest I came to major rebellion was a ridiculous amount of eye-rolling and snickering, some short-lived school-skipping sessions, and a brief "gang stint," which only lasted three hours due to the fact that I was too chicken to let the so-called "leaders" slice my finger open with the edge of a Coke can for the blood initiation ceremony. More than twenty years later (let's skip the exact math) I decided to do all the stuff I wish I had done back then just to torture my hubby, including partying with my girlfriends, dressing inappropriately, sulking, indulging in self-pity, having a phone attached to my ear at all times, getting some piercings and a radical haircut, experimenting with drugs (only the occasional Valium when needed), and generally behaving irresponsibly, like forgetting to feed the cat, spending money I don't have, and inviting my friends over to hang out and eat everything in the fridge! When my husband tried to interfere, I yelled, "You're not the boss of me!" and almost burst out laughing at his reaction. He was so shocked he just stood there, eyes bulging, nose flaring, and said: "What are you? A teenager?"

My response? "Yes. Yes I am."

Chapter Four

SLOW TORTURE

61 *Nag Him Endlessly*

The definition of nagging is probably enough to send your man into panic-attack mode, so let's begin with a clear understanding of the verb. According-ing to the *American Heritage Dictionary*, to nag is to annoy by constant scolding, complaining, or urging. It also means to torment persistently, as with anxiety or pain.

RISK INDICATOR: 1
You're In the Clear
What can we say? Nagging is in our DNA, right? Enjoy every delicious drop!

Women are constantly being accused of doing this already (although I tend to disagree, because I'd rather ignore my husband completely than even bother nagging him), but as we've already been wrongly labeled since the dawn of time, let's just go with it!

Pester, annoy, and NAG YOUR MAN TO MADNESS whenever possible.

Remind him of all the crap he needs to do. Tell him how he prom-ised to mow the lawn, call his mother, finish all those annoying little projects he's been meaning to get to, build that tree house for the kids, help the neighbors with their landscaping, clean the cars, take the dog to the vet. You can seriously nag all day when you get into it. Try this for a test run:

Good morning sweetie. What can I make you for breakfast? Oh, eggs and bacon?

Well honey, you know Dr. Yang wants you to lose thirty pounds, so I think you should have some fresh fruit and healthy cereal instead. In fact, wouldn't it be great if you went for a run before breakfast? Exercise does a body good, and you don't exercise like you used to, sweetie, which isn't good. Speaking of things that aren't good, you haven't been very nice to your mother these days. She's been calling you constantly and wants you to go by her house, but you just keep ignoring her. It's not nice to ignore your mother. She's so good to you and you should try being a better son. When was the last time you spent some quality time with her? She really misses you. You know, you should drop by and see her this weekend, but not tomorrow because you need to finish cleaning up the garage and you've been putting it off for weeks. Ya know, every day that goes by is a wasted day, sweetheart. That reminds me, the children need your help with their science projects. Honestly, I really don't know where your time goes! You should really do something about that. I should pick up a great book for you Sally told me about. It helps procrastinators get their act together. You could really use it. Oh, you're doing something later? With who? When? Where? What time will you be done? Don't forget you need to run some errands for me when you're finished.

Just one day of hard-core nagging, and your hubby will be checking into the nearest hotel! If you need help, just channel Alice from *The Honeymooners* and go crazy with it. (It's no wonder Ralph Kramden would threaten to send her "to the moon!" Her nasally voice could make *anyone's* ears bleed.) Or think about Edith Bunker from *All In The Family.* For the younger set, you can channel Peggy Bundy from *Married with Children,* and add some whining along with the relentless nagging. By the end of the day your husband will have either gotten plenty of work done just to shut you up, or packed his bags. You win regardless.

62 Forget His Birthday

Men always act like they don't care about significant dates like birthdays and anniversaries, but God forbid you neglect to mark HIS special day with a massive gift, intricate plans, or a friggin' parade. He's traumatized for life!

RISK INDICATOR: 2
Caution, Girlfriend
Remember, payback is a bitch, and you want some jewelry for your next birthday, don't you? Proceed with caution.

No matter what, birthdays will always carry special significance, and no one wants to be forgotten on his birthday, even if it's simply marked with a card or a phone call.

So how did the tradition of "birthday celebrating" actually begin? Some speculate the tradition started centuries ago in Europe where people believed evil spirits would try to harm birthday celebrants. Hoping to scare off those naughty demons, family and friends spent the day eating and dancing with the birthday guy or gal, thus keeping any evil spirits from crashing the party.

Regardless of its origin, birthday traditions have endured and are still considered a big deal across the globe, which is why simply "forgetting" his birthday is a perfect torture maneuver! Now, you must be strong and show absolutely no interest if he happens to bring up his birthday for any reason. Just say something vague like "Yeah . . . I'm working on that," and quickly walk away when the issue comes up. This is crucial because you can't get involved in any detailed birthday conversations if you really want to pull off the prank in a perfect way!

Birthday Execution Plan: Wake up that morning and go about your day without saying a word! Acting completely normal is key . . . he'll be utterly baffled! If it happens to be a weekend, leave the house as soon as you can, claiming you have to run some bogus errand—he'll think you're doing some secret birthday stuff, so he'll play along. If it's a weekday, then it's off to work, where you'll be sure to be busy busy busy all day—allowing you to miss his panicked phone call wondering how you could have possibly committed the serious offense of forgetting his big day! Note: If your husband happens to confront you before you can even leave the house, and says something like "Hey, you're not even gonna say happy birthday?" shrug your shoulders and just say "Oh sweetie, I've been so busy with (insert any of the following: the kids, housework, big project for work), I didn't even have a chance to think about it! Oh well, there's always next year!"

63 Plan a Major Home Renovation

As a big fan of ABC's *Extreme Makeover: Home Edition*, I know there is nothing better than having your home completely remodeled, re-fangled, and refurnished—as long as you're not doing it yourself or paying for it out of your pocket (or 401[k] plan). It is my experience that all remodeling projects have two things in common:

> **RISK INDICATOR: 4**
> *Watch Your Back*
> Don't send yourself up shit creek without a paddle. Keep an eye on your budget, and remember: the more you spend on that home renovation project, the less you'll have left over for your next girlie getaway!

1. They will *never* come in under budget.
2. They will take at least twice as long as originally planned.

I don't need to tell you how men can't stand to spend buttloads of money on unnecessary crap, and you and I both know that when women come up with a plan to do a little tinkering around the house, it's almost always crap you don't really need to do, or crap you just feel like doing because you have nothing else to do. This will make your man want to strangle you with electrical tape, so let's proceed, and plan to inconvenience him as much as humanly possible. Dens or offices are quite often a man's domain (where husbands like to go to hide out and detox when they've had enough of the madness going on around them), so destroying that sanctuary sounds like the perfect place to start, if you ask me!

Once you decide you are going to tear down some walls and expand your husband's favorite space, the next step is deciding what you will do with the new area. Should you install a fully equipped home theater with authentic seating and giant screen? A gym would be nice, a playroom for the kids, or an elegant sunroom for reading and relaxing. Your husband might actually be receptive to the idea of adding a luxurious bar with plenty of space for a pool table (which could be fun for the whole family) but he'll hate the fact that he'll be without his sanctuary for however long it takes for your extensive plan to come together. Not to mention how outrageously expensive this whole thing will be. As with any home demolition—er, revision—once the mission gets under way, it's like a freight train barreling through, forcing all kinds of violent and unexpected changes. I mean, if you're already expanding the room, why not tear up the old carpeting and put down shockingly expensive hardwood floors? Plus the walls will absolutely require a fresh coat of paint—they'll look dull once the shiny new floor is down—which makes perfect sense to me! While you're at it, update the lighting fixtures and go with some outrageously expensive design (which is really easy to do because when it comes to electrical configuring, a quick visit from a licensed electrician can cost you an arm, a leg, and several ribs, too!). Don't forget, kitchens and bathrooms are usually the most expensive rooms to update (because of the added cost of appliances, and marble, should you go that route), but it's up to you where to make your changes. No matter what you decide to go with, be sure your man will not be thrilled. Don't worry, though; he can use your mounting bills to wipe away his tears.

64 Join a Cult

There's just something about cults that just leads to trouble. Am I right? Why can't people just join a fan club, or become a simple supporter of a group? What drives folks to want to become official "cult members?" Is it something they always thought of doing?

> **RISK INDICATOR: 3**
> *He Might Be On to You*
> Most of us are level-headed enough to steer clear of the acid-laced Kool-Aid, so your husband may not buy the whole dog-and-pony show. Everyone, though, can use some Mary Kay Mineral Bronzing Powder. It does miracles for a sallow complexion!

Or did they just wake up one morning and think, "Ya know, I kinda like the idea of worshipping some guy with a wacky beard and a massive superiority complex who thinks we should drink some funny-tasting juice all the time and frolic around naked in this place he calls the commune. No, it doesn't bother me that he might be a little psychotic. So what? We're all a little crazy from time to time. Listen, he seems really nice actually, and he's always smiling despite that swastika on his forehead. Hey, maybe that's a new trend! Yep, this sounds like my kind of fun. I've done my research. Sign me up!"

Who knows, maybe it does happen like that. So I guess it's pretty easy to join a cult. The upside is you'll definitely have lots of new friends, that's for sure.

What kind of cults are out there now? Since most cult movements end in a fiery death (Waco) or long-term imprisonment (Manson) or beaming up to a nonexistent spaceship via suicide (Heaven's Gate), they usually aren't around for long, but don't you worry, new and even creepier cults emerge daily to take their place! If we're going to give our husbands an ulcer over this, let's find a phenomenal cult with all the right ingredients (including extreme religious views, a crazed leader, exaggerated promises, restricted freedoms, and systematic deception) guaranteed to rock your hubby's world, or at the very least give it a good rattling!

Let's start with the basics. If you're taking the "religious cult" route, you've got a massive array of choices, with the most popular ones being the Church of Scientology, Satanism, and good ol' Jehovah's Witnesses. (Can I get an AMEN?) Moving on to "hate cults," you've got your standard Ku Klux Klan, militia groups, and Islamic extremists (for fans of suicide bombings). Then we have "political and psychological cults" such as the Spartacist League and the Silva Method (which I hear yields great results!). Of course, doomsday cults are still very popular and may or may not involve religious teachings. However, most generally rely on "millennialism" (the thought that critical dates will bring the fulfillment of their beliefs). These cults include the Seven Seals (the artists formerly known as the Branch Davidians), the Order of the Solar Temple, and Aum Shinrykio (for the Japanese cult aficionado). And finally, we have the most insidious groups in the brainwashing cult world: "commercial cults," a.k.a. multilevel marketing schemes such as Amway, Herbalife, and Mary Kay (yes, you there with the pink Cadillac and matching pink tote full of recruitment forms!).

So many cults and just one brain to control . . . which will you choose? Whichever you go with, consider your husband your number one recruitment target!

65 *Declare a Chick-Flick Week*

This particular punishment happens to be one of my favorites because I'm a self-diagnosed chick-flick addict, and my husband (who totally denies crying during *Beaches* even though he used all my tissues) loathes even the thought of

RISK INDICATOR: 3
He Might Be On to You
Don't let your guard down. He might make a run for it when he sees the girls pulling up! Lockdown is suggested.

being subjected to high levels of estrogen in the form of film—and would rather "stick needles in his retina" than watch female bonding on the big or small screen. Declaring a chick-flick week in my house is equivalent to declaring a full-scale war—and boy, do I enjoy the battle. Imagine an entire week of tearjerking favorites, getting more and more emotionally draining night after night! The drama will drain your man's energy like kryptonite does Superman's! Of course, you want to make sure that if you are getting ready to declare a full-scale chick-flick week you will be absolutely victorious, so preparing ahead of time is of utmost importance. Scour your local video store (or your online video provider) for the cream of the crop. Not all chick flicks achieve the high level of emotional drainage and tear-inducing magic that we want for this exceptional occasion. So as you search for the best of the best you might want to stock up on these heartwarming classics: *Breakfast at Tiffany's*, *Casablanca*, *The Way We Were*, and *An Affair to Remember*. Or, you can pick up some of my all-time female favorites, like *Steel Magnolias*, *The First Wives Club*, *When Harry Met Sally*, *Legends of the Fall*, *My Best Friend's Wedding*, *Ghost*, *The Bridges of Madison County*, *Pretty Woman*, *Sleepless in Seattle*, *Mystic Pizza*, *Thelma and Louise*, *Titanic*, *Bridget Jones's Diary*, *Moulin Rouge*, *The Notebook*, and the list goes on and on! We all have our favorites, so these are just some great titles you might want to consider. Set the scene with lots of cozy throw pillows, whip up some comforting chamomile tea, and don't forget the extra-large boxes of tissue, which you will definitely need—except he'll be crying for a whole different reason! Make sure to periodically ask your man annoying questions during the movie:

Do you love me as much as he loves her? Do you think they'll make it in the end? If I die, would you long for me endlessly?

To really send him over the edge, invite your entire "girl crew" over to share in the magical evening, but save the best spot on the couch for your favorite guy, who will be begging for mercy before the credits roll on your first flick of the evening!

PROOF POSITIVE

A study conducted at the University of Alberta says men are much more likely to enjoy "chick flicks" if they know they're watching a fictional story. Women, on the other hand, generally have a higher level of empathy than men and tend to enjoy a story more when they know it is based on fact. The findings were published in the February 2008 issue of the *Journal of Consumer Research.*

66 Volunteer Him for the School Field Trip

If your husband thought the "playdate" was the worst day of his life (see Chapter 3, #43), just wait till he sees his name on the parent volunteer list for the upcoming class field trip! This kind of fun should be outlawed,

RISK INDICATOR: 1
You're in the Clear

Let me reiterate. It is high time daddies get more involved and suffer along with the rest of us who are subjected to school volunteer torture on a regular basis. Welcome to the responsible parent club!

but you can (and will) get away with it because you are only encouraging fatherly involvement, which is a stipulation of the overall parental contract. (That sounds pretty official, doesn't it?) There should really be no room for argument in this scenario. Fair is fair, and can you honestly remember the last time you husband even set foot at your child's school? Does he even know where it is? Well, draw him a map, girlfriend, and get him on that bus to crazyland.

Maybe I missed the memo. Have fathers been banned from field trips and school volunteering? When did this become only a mother's domain? Ah yes, after attending countless "cutie patootie" school events (and racking up more volunteer hours than the PTA president) you have earned the right to strike a balance. No more excuses, Daddy. The buck (and any other paper currency) stops here.

Your child needs to know Mommy is not the only parent who cares enough to spend the day with a bunch of rugrats. Daddy is just as happy to cancel his all-important appointments and leave his quiet office (kicking and screaming) to share some memorable moments with the apple of his eye.

What makes this situation all the more enjoyable is the fact that he'll most likely be the only dad there, thrust into a foreign and unpredictable world. But don't you worry about him. Your child's teacher and the other "power moms" will whip him into shape in no time. Before you know it he'll be in the thick of it, sifting through a sea of complicated permission slips, passing out nametags, assigning partners, breaking up partner fights, checking the emergency kit, securing snacks and lunch boxes, breaking up more fights, and finally boarding the big yellow bus that will whisk the wild bunch to the museum, movie, zoo, puppet show, park, kid concert, campsite, or wherever the heck they've secured space to park the bus and then spending two to four hours repeating safety rules and shuttling germ-infested, noisy kids (including your own) to and from the bathroom.

Keep in mind that field trips are all about exposing children to new things and stimulating their natural curiosity, so you know what that means . . . the questions will be unleashed with rapid-fire force, and no one is safe. Why were the monkeys kissing? How do snakes go to the bathroom? Is global warming going to kill us all?

If your husband survives the journey he'll certainly gain perspective, and have a newfound respect for the great job you do. Just a one-time field trip experience will provide years of sympathy, and possibly recurring nightmares.

67 Make Cracks about His Gray

Ahhh, going gray—the sure sign that you're not fifteen anymore. While a limited number of men actually look incredibly sexy with a gray noggin (think Sean Connery, Richard Gere, and George Clooney), graying is not a welcome change for 99.9 percent of the testosterone crew. Let's face it, gray hair is just a few

> **RISK INDICATOR: 1**
> *You're in the Clear*
> Every man should expect to be teased about his silver strands; it's his official entrée into real manhood.

steps away from wearing Depends and lining up for early-bird specials, so most likely, your hubby will be pretty sensitive to comments like, "Wow, you're really starting to really look like your Dad," or "You know, that Grecian Formula works pretty well, and it's easy to use!"

My husband totally refuses to stop wearing hair gel because he's starting to go gray, and he hates the idea of "showing his age" (apparently he doesn't realize his wrinkles kinda blow his cover) but anyhow, we could seriously end world hunger with all the moola men spend on delaying the inevitable. Gray hair just happens. There is nothing you can do. Accept it and move on. But for those who have ever wondered why we actually go gray, here's some quick 411: Research reveals hair turns gray as we age when the follicles at the base of the hair shaft cease to produce melanin (your natural hair pigment/color). Each follicle contains a limited number of pigment cells. With age, the pigment cells in the follicle gradually die off. As they do so, each hair strand no longer contains as much color and will show up as silver, gray, or white as it grows. Eventually, all the pigment cells die and the hair becomes completely gray. It can take ten years or more to complete the entire process!

But what about the age-old notion that "stress" causes gray strands? Every parent on the planet would say stress is definitely a factor connected to graying hair because, Lord knows, most of the time those suckers don't show up until kids do. However, according to *Scientific American*, while stress hormones may have some impact on hair color (taking a toll on melanin production) there is still no clear link between stress and gray hair. As luck would have it however, sudden stress (which interrupts the body's natural rhythm) IS linked to HAIR LOSS, causing hair follicles to fall out and revert to a resting phase. Examples of this include surgery, severe dieting, book writing . . . but luckily, "stress balding" is only temporary and eventually the hair will grow back, ironically making it susceptible to the graying process! Now here's my big secret—I happen to think my hubby looks sizzlin' hot with his salt and pepper strands, only I would never DREAM of congratulating him on his gray. (I have too much fun torturing him about it!) So go forth and get crazy with the gray. It wouldn't hurt to buy him some handy "hair lipstick" (for temporary touchups) to really drive the issue home.

68 *Badger Him about His Bald Spot*

To continue the theme, we *all* know there's also nothing a man dreads more than losing his hair, so if this is the case with your guy, go straight for his sore spot and let loose on his bald spot! It will be especially bothersome if someone else is around to hear you make fun of the naked patch on your hubby's head, so try to make that happen if

RISK INDICATOR: 2
Caution, Girlfriend
He may not take too kindly to your jokes and decide to purchase some pricey hair plugs. Unfortunately, he'll end up looking like an alien and you still have to take him to parties. Consider carefully.

possible. Here are some creative comments you can use. Believe me, even Mr. Baldy will think they're funny.

- "Sweetie, the 'Hair Club for Men' called—they'd like to have a word with you."
- "I had to hire a plumber because your fuzz keeps clogging up the tub!"
- "You must be saving a ton on haircuts now!"
- "There's a hat sale at Macy's. I'll pick some up for you."
- "Can I start calling you 'Mr. Clean' now?"
- "Honey, that commercial for 'Magic Spray Hair' is on again, come quick!"
- "I guess borrowing a comb is out of the question now?"
- "Just in case you're interested, they're holding local auditions for *The King and I*."
- "Let me get my sunglasses, the glare from your head is blinding!"
- "Got Rogaine?"

Honestly, I don't know why men freak out so much about losing their hair. It's not something they can control, so why be embarrassed about it? Obviously, they feel like it ages them prematurely . . . but unless you're sportin' a shiny bald spot when you're thirteen, it shouldn't be any cause for alarm. Of course, men don't feel this way, because it's happening to them and not me (I guess I would be a little perturbed if my locks suddenly decided to jump ship), so maybe I understand why the panic eventually sets in. Recently, I decided to do my own Random Balding Stranger Survey (RBSS) while I was at the mall and the results were pretty much what I expected! I approached several obviously balding strangers and asked them if they were sensitive about their missing hair. About 85 percent admitted they usually don't even think about the issue—until someone brings it up, and then they feel awkward and humiliated. In the end, my research revealed the hair-raising truth about men and their locks. They usually take it for granted till it takes a hike; then it becomes a hairy situation (pardon the pun).

PROOF POSITIVE

If bald is really beautiful, why is it that Americans spend $1 billion a year in hair restoration treatments? Research shows more than 50 percent of men are affected by baldness by the age of fifty, so if your husband hasn't lost his manly strands yet, chances are he will eventually. Be patient, and make generous offerings to the hair gods.

69 Whine about Wanting a Bigger Diamond

Diamonds are a girl's best friend and a man's worst enemy.—AUTHOR UNKNOWN

The diamond solitaire. So simple, yet so complicated.

Before a diamond solitaire floats into your life, you are a single woman with a dream. You visualize your idyllic future filled with love

RISK INDICATOR: 2
Caution, Girlfriend
He might think you are just a spoiled brat and decide he's never going to buy you any jewelry again, a thought too sad to ponder.

and laughter, as well as the perfect man at your side. A man whose smile fills your heart with immeasurable joy, a man who worships you, a man you want to spend the rest of your life with, whose children you can't wait to bear, and whose hand you want to hold even when you are too old to remember the exact date and time when he put a ring on your finger and asked you to be his wife.

Engagement rings are so significant. That hunk of carbon mounted on a round piece of metal becomes the ultimate symbol of passionate devotion between two people and a promise of beautiful things to come. If we only knew what really happens afterward, no woman would ever settle for anything less than England's priceless Crown Jewels.

Of course, when two people decide to get married, they may not be in a position to be able to afford such grandeur. Well, let's be honest. "He" may not be in the ideal financial situation to afford a superb jewel for his beloved, so he obtains what is in his reach at the time, and such silly girls are we that we take whatever comes our way regardless of carat, cut, color, and clarity (the determining four C's).

Further down the road—and several kids and stretch marks later—a wife sits in her kitchen admiring her minuscule and ordinary engagement ring. She's a bit melancholy, wondering where all the time (and passion) has gone, thinking of all the sacrifices she's had to make, mourning the body she used to have wishing she could still sleep till noon, and it's all because she accepted this tiny diamond during a nervous proposal. Then she suddenly realizes . . . her husband can now afford a bigger diamond! After all her patience and tolerance, she'll finally get the rock she always wanted, and has now truly earned after dealing with her man for more than a decade! So how will she get that rock? She will whine like a child and force her husband into submission. We all know a little whine before dinner is just divine, so she waits for her husband to get home from a long day's work, when she proceeds to pounce on him like a hungry cheetah. "Honey, can I please upgrade my engagement ring and get a bigger diamond?? Please? Please? Please? Please? Please? Why not? We've been married forever and I still have sex with you! C'mon, baby, pleeeezzzee! Whhyyy not???? Please honey . . . Don't you love meeee? PLEASE! PLEASE! PLEASE! It's not fair. Pleeeeaaassseeee?? I'll cry forever if I have to . . . Puleeezzzeeeeee??" I assure you that after a few days of this your husband will give in, or his head will explode. For the record, whining is only acceptable when you are trying to convince your husband to buy you a bigger piece of highly concentrated carbon.

70 Post His Picture on a Gay Dating Website

Allow me to make a massive sweeping generalization here. All heterosexual male *Homo sapiens* would be UTTERLY MORTIFIED at the thought of their picture posted on a gay dating website (even as a joke). They would not only feel completely

> **RISK INDICATOR: 5**
> *Run Like Hell*
> Never underestimate a straight male whose reputation has been shattered. Consider him dangerous, and possibly armed.

violated but would cringe at the idea of being displayed like a giant slab of meat to a hungry den of lions (just dying to taste their sexy man flesh). This torture is such a stroke of genius, even my straight male friends (who can't believe I am writing this book) had to hand it to me for being so damn creative! Can you honestly think of any worst punishment or torture? Well, I'm sure you can, but this one is particularly clever because your guy may truly never know about it—unless you decide to show him his matches, flirts, and/or intriguing propositions.

It sounds meaner than it is. Really, so what if millions of gay men will be salivating at the thought of getting their hands on your man's heinie, maybe might print his picture and do unspeakable things with it, and/or some of his friends might actually get wind of said posting and kick him out of the straight boys club. Big deal. It's just a little harmless joke. No biggie.

Okay, it may be a bit of a biggie for him, but it's all in the name of good, clean fun! Or at least that's what you'll say if and when you get busted. So where do you start? Well the answer is pretty darn simple. You can do a quick web search for "gay dating websites" and start looking through the plethora of gay partnering sites that abound. I happened to go a step further when I considered doing this for kicks, so I asked one of my nearest and dearest gay pals where he goes for the ultimate gay hook-up. He was more than happy to provide these marvelous websites for our viewing pleasure. I highly recommend you check these out whether you torture your hubby this way or not. The scenery is highly entertaining, incredibly educational, and frankly, all dating websites should be so darn liberal with their photo rules and regulations. Yowza! Should you choose to have a little fun and put up your man's profile, these sites also happen to be completely FREE, so that's definitely a plus, girlfriend. Check out these jaw-dropping sites:

- *www.gaywatch.com*
- *www.lifeout.com*
- *www.adam4adam.com*
- *www.gaydar.com*
- *www.manhunt.net*

I happen to adore the Manhunt site 'cause they cover tons of diverse selections for any palate, offering foreign male options in *Français*, *Português*, and *Deutsch*. The only thing you might want to do (just to save your own ass should he find out) is give him a phony name and don't post any real personal information like addresses and phone numbers. Protecting his true identity is key, especially if he becomes top gay hottie of the month!

PROOF POSITIVE

From the Internet Dating Guide: Is web dating popular? According to the latest research, there are more than 85 million single American adults and two out of five have tried online dating. That's well over 30 million! Meanwhile, a study by ComScore found that dating sites attract more than 30 million visitors a month in the United States alone!

71 Drag Him to Marriage Counseling

Counseling always sounds like a yucky word. Say it with me . . . C O U N S E L I N G almost sounds like D Y I N G, but definitely with a better end result I guess.

Things are usually not too good if you are seeking "counsel" (unless you need advice on what to do with your $2 billion trust fund). Counseling is most

RISK INDICATOR: 2
Caution, Girlfriend
Counseling can take you to many unforeseen places. Once you open the door, get ready for some eye-opening discoveries.

likely the last place you end up before something goes really wrong. When you seek counseling as a couple you are admitting to some type of failure, you've hit a brick wall, and you really need guidance. There's got to be some tumultuous trouble in paradise when you go out of your way to request third-party involvement. Chances are, if you're reading this book you've probably considered marriage counseling at some point, or you're currently in the throes of it, but that's perfectly acceptable, and the first step toward recovery, so welcome, grab a seat, and let's chat.

Women are always much better at the counseling thing because there's nothing women love more than talking and venting, and having an audience willing to listen to our rants makes it even better. If you think about it, we women start therapy as children, confiding in our dolls, then our siblings, and eventually our girlfriends. If we're lucky, our husbands will have the patience to listen to all of our dramas without slitting their wrists in the process. Conversely, men are not born talkers and think discussing their problems is a sign of weakness, so they generally keep things to themselves, eventually working out problems on their own or ignoring issues altogether until they just go away completely unresolved. For men, being dragged off to counseling is like forcing a child to eat his vegetables. They will kick and scream the whole way through—and hate you more every time you make them do it.

Other than cheating, forcing men to discuss marital problems with a total stranger (no matter what degrees or licenses he or she holds) is the ultimate form of betrayal.

For those who've experienced counseling, isn't it funny how husbands constantly give you the dismayed "I can't believe you're talking about that" look even though airing out your dirty laundry is exactly what you're SUPPOSED to do when you're in counseling? My husband hated our therapy sessions so much he relentlessly tried to negotiate his way out of them. I was offered all kinds of great stuff . . . cruises, jewelry, *anything* to get out of the torture of sitting on that ugly leather couch and facing the music. I really got him good when I booked double sessions without any warning. Emergency sessions are even more exciting. And when fights crop up, make him suffer by saying the following words: "I can't wait to hear what our therapist says about this on Monday!" Just threatening therapy is enough to make him behave better, but take it from me, even the happiest couples can benefit from some time on the couch.

72 Go for a Total Makeover

I get so excited just thinking about this I could squeal! I haven't had extensive plastic surgery aside from a little lipo and some pre-emptive Botox, but I fully support the "makeover movement"—as long as you're not cashing in your kids' college fund to finance

RISK INDICATOR: 2
Caution, Girlfriend
Word of advice: don't become a human Barbie doll. In this case, less is definitely more.

your breast implants. With that said, however, there is always the extreme, and going there is never a good idea. A little nip and tuck to boost your self-esteem is one thing; turning yourself into a walking science experiment is quite another. I can honestly say I always planned to grow old gracefully (and thought physical vanity was appalling) until the day I had a baby, and woke up attached to someone else's body. I thought maybe the "deflated balloon thing" my stomach was doing was temporary. As the months went by, I convinced myself the wrinkled flesh flap that now hung over my underwear would somehow just disappear with proper diet and exercise. Years later I still fantasize about lopping it off with an office paper cutter.

What I'm trying to say is that no one should be judged for trying to look and feel better—as long as you do it in a sterile environment with a board-certified plastic surgeon. At this point you are probably wondering how a tummy tuck or some bigger ta-tas would torture your husband. Here's how: While your hubby might aesthetically enjoy the "new you," he'll hate the fact that other men will also enjoy taking in the view, and even the most secure husband will slowly be consumed with jealousy and have paranoid fears of you running off with "RRRRoberto," your new, sexy, twenty-five-year-old Brazilian personal trainer.

Let there be no confusion though. I am in no way encouraging women to go out and get massive, painful, and risky reconstructive plastic surgery (unless you really want to). That is a very personal choice, and surgery is never something to be entered into blindly (or even remotely cloudy-eyed). Not to mention the fact that these procedures ain't cheap! Your average boob job will set you back a couple grand, and tummy tucks (while shockingly effective in curing flesh-flap syndrome) can run you about six large.

As I said, I haven't had plastic surgery yet, but I've done my personal version of a total makeover, doing some minor facial "rejuvenating" (scalpel-free and very subtle), losing enough body fat to fill the Gulf of Mexico, and you also can say my hair looks a little different these days (courtesy of some quality hair extensions). I was pretty pleased with my "refreshening," but I had no idea my husband would turn into a raving lunatic. Suddenly he went from yawning when I stripped naked to saying things like, "Isn't that skirt a little too short?" and "You didn't even look this good when I married you!" Yep, he's crazy jealous now, it's torture for him, and it's been really cathartic for me. I always heard looking good is the best revenge, but now I know it's true, and hopefully so will you!

73 *Engage in Crazy Talk*

The difference between genius and insanity is that genius has its limits.—ALBERT EINSTEIN

RISK INDICATOR: 1
You're in the Clear
Everyone does their share of "crazy talking" once in a while . . . but make it a habit and it's sure to keep your guy on his toes!

(Note: Some names have been changed to protect the innocent and conserve long-term, meaningful friendships.)

My friend Sherri is a few threads short of a sweater. Her husband, Rob, truly adores his eccentric wife (and I also adore her), but Sherri does tend to say some pretty zany things from time to time, and it seriously drives her husband absolutely raving mad! He's told me on several occasions he's always questioned Sherri's mental state, but I bet all the curry in India that Sherri is not certifiable, she just knows how to push her hubby's buttons, and does it with delightful passive-aggressive grace and style. We have come to refer to Sherri's hilarious outbursts simply as "Sherri-isms." Here are a few of the funnier ones for you to enjoy:

- "The dog has to go to the vet, he's got his period again."
- "I swear the phone rings inconsistently all day long!"
- "I had to buy a new couch because the old one was just too comfortable!"
- "Honestly, I feel sorry for Aileen Wuornos, she was just misunderstood."

- "Ya know, my physic warned me about this."
- "Just because I talk to my toaster doesn't mean I'm crazy!"

Now you can see why Sherri's husband needs intense therapy. But "crazy talk" is definitely a deliciously funny and unusual way to mess with your man's mind. Entertain yourself by making up your very own "isms." Come up with strange and somewhat threatening statements like, "Geez, if I only had an industrial-sized bottle of bleach, the things I could do." Your husband will be afraid. Very afraid.

Of course, my pal Sherri isn't the only human in existence who has ever engaged in bizarre "crazy talk," so for fun, I've included some of the more amusing celebrity "crazy talk" quotes here, in no particular order:

- **Ozzy Osbourne:** "Being sober on a bus is, like, totally different than being drunk on a bus."
- **Tara Reid:** "I had a ghost named John that lived in my house. I didn't, like, hang out with him, I just saw him."
- **George W. Bush:** "You teach a child to read and he or her will be able to pass a literacy test."
- **Liam Gallagher:** "I'm a tender, loving, and beautiful guy who tends to slap a photographer now and then."
- **Lindsay Lohan:** "I love being in the car and not going anywhere. I trick my friends . . . they'll be like, 'Where are we going?'"

74 Go Green 'til He Screams

We all know taking care of the environment is the thing to do to ensure our beautiful planet doesn't implode blah, blah, blah, but some people take it just a wee bit too far, like for example my mother, who actually washes and reuses paper towels! Look, no one can escape the "go green" message, and I completely understand the team-effort mentality when it comes to

RISK INDICATOR: 1
You're in the Clear
What kind of ignoramus could possibly fault you for caring about the environment? Its not easy being green, but making your husband scream will be worth the effort.

environmental issues. Yes, every single person should pitch in and do their share, so why not take advantage of the message, push the green envelope, AND seriously annoy our husbands at the same time?

You can start by "talking green" every single chance you get. Become utterly consumed with saving "Mother Earth," make it your mission to constantly remind everyone to "think green" at all times, and proselytize till your husband pulls his hair out! We all know men enjoy incessant nitpicking and nagging, so you'll be on the right track from the very beginning. The next step is to hold an intense "green gathering" in your home—a family meeting to discuss what all members should be doing to support the cause. Proudly announce how you've already started buying environmentally friendly cleaning products (or making them out of vinegar and locally grown organic herbs), how your baby is now wearing only biodegradable disposable diapers (which must be specially ordered and cost twice as much as regular diapers), and how you've found a way to avoid wasting thousands of gallons of water by simply forsaking the washing machine and "recycling" your family's soiled clothing with Refresh'n Dryer Towels! At this point your husband will want to choke you with organic rope, but that's when you turn to him and give him a long list of the eco-changes he'll have to make literally overnight (a challenge he'll be up for when he realizes you'll be on him like Al Gore on car emissions.)

Grudgingly, he'll accept your outrageous green demands (and may even agree to trade in his evil gas-guzzling SUV monster for the most reasonable electric car he can find), but he will surely put his foot down when he discovers your "greening crusade" will even affect the way you two "get down to business."

According to planetgreen.com and sister site treehugger.com, there are various enlightening ways to connect romantically without killing the environment, and to welcome eco-savvy changes into your bedroom while enhancing your lovemaking the natural way. Oh yeah, we're talking all-natural organic lube, bamboo bed sheets, rechargeable batteries for your sex toys, biodegradable condoms (the jury is still out on whether that's actually possible), and even sexy "eco-undies" guaranteed to provide a "tilt in his kilt" (as long as that kilt is made from 100 percent recycled fibers!). And we all know a healthy environment is only made better when it is coupled with eco-conscious eating. Just wait till he finds out he'll also be in charge of the family garden, featuring only pesticide-free produce!

75 *Spend Quality Time with the Mother-in-Law*

I know few people who have massive affection or incredible tolerance for their in-laws. Mothers-in-law are especially difficult to deal with because:

RISK INDICATOR: 3
He Might Be On to You
Keep track of your lies, or you might find yourself spending quality time with *his* mother as payback.

1. She's not your mother.
2. You are only related because you happened to marry her offspring.
3. Your own mother tends to drive you batty, so inheriting another mother isn't exactly a banner moment.

Some men (God bless them) are great with their mothers-in-law; the other 99.9 percent of them just deal with their wives' mothers because they have no choice. It has always perplexed me how a man can completely fall in love with a woman and then so strongly dislike the woman she came from. Then again, it's no different for me. My mother-in-law is no picnic in Central Park, but her son I happened to fall madly in love with and marry. It is these kinds of puzzling life questions that keep me up late at night. As for this mother-in-law–induced torture exercise, it really helps to determine whether your husband and your mother are on speaking terms. If your answer is a "no," hide the knives, skip to another section, and come back when your mom and your husband are on civil terms again.

If your answer is a "yes," let's proceed. Your challenge is to figure out how to get those two to spend a chunk of time together and send your husband into violent convulsions. I've actually achieved this monumental feat on several occasions. How, you ask? Here's my secret. I lie my ass off.

For example, my mother doesn't like leaving the two-mile radius of her neighborhood too often, but on occasion she is forced to travel far beyond her boundaries to the outskirts of town; i.e., the mall, where she will spend an entire day comparison shopping before she actually purchases a single item. My mom always gives me major advance notice for these special events, so that's when I start plotting, and then I set my plan in motion. On the appointed day, I tell my husband I have plans to take my mom to the mall. He's immediately thrilled because he knows that neither of us will be around to nag him all day, so he makes his own plans, and thinks life is just grand. What he doesn't know is that I've made arrangements with one of my girlfriends to call me with some sudden emergency, something like she has to take one of her kids to the hospital for swallowing a penny, and needs me to stay with the others (this actually happened once, so it's totally plausible). You rush off, telling your husband he now has to take your mom to the mall because she's already dressed and waiting to be picked up. Sixteen hours later he'll return with a headache as big as Mount Rushmore, and a newfound appreciation for assisted suicide. Getting these archenemies together isn't easy, but the end result is worth every bit of effort.

Now that I've given you the general plan, go forward and conquer!

76 *Live Out Your Singing Dreams*

Average price of a karaoke machine: **$300**

Days of the week you can use it: **7**

The look on your husband's face: **Priceless**

So you can't make it on *American Idol*? Never fear! You can hold your very own *American Idol* wannabe competition in the privacy of your own acoustically challenged home! It's a great way to get the kids involved, and make it a highly entertaining family event. So your hus-

RISK INDICATOR: 1

You're in the Clear

He can run, but he can't hide! Karaoke is good, clean family fun. He'll have no choice but to participate!

band's ears will bleed? So what! He'll have fun while he's at it, and don't even let him think he's just going to be a spectator; he's expected to perform regularly, with grace and precise execution. Once you fork over the money for quality karaoke equipment, you'll want to put it to good use, so plug in that mic, and get ready for a real show. How about a nightly competition? Weekly is fine too, and monthly will have to do if you have no choice (I know, homework and dishes still need to get done). But the point of this is just having a blast, and forcing your husband to have a blast too, even if he whines and cries actual tears while enduring it.

Karaoke is a funny word, isn't it? I decided to do a little research, and found that the term is actually a combination of two Japanese words: *kara*, meaning "empty," and *oke*, which is short for *okesutura*, meaning "orchestra." I also was pretty surprised to find out karaoke wasn't developed by my favorite *American Idol* judge, Simon Cowell, but is believed to have originated about twenty years ago in a Japanese bar where the house band recorded its music onto tape, and when they couldn't make it to a performance (too busy watching *Godzilla* movies, no doubt) bar patrons filled in, and sang along to the recorded tunes. Soon the news spread to other bars, whose owners immediately replaced their house bands with recorded music and invited drunken patrons to sing onstage and embarrass themselves in public, while they pocketed the money they would have been dishing out for actual talented musicians. Since then, karaoke has become a true phenomenon, sweeping the entire continent, and even producing national and international karaoke singing contests with big-money winners. Tell your husband he could be one of the success stories, and at the very least, he can scare the neighbors with a screaming rendition of Queen's "Bohemian Rhapsody." C'mon, who could turn that down? And don't forget how adorably painful it is to hear your children belt out classics like "The Wheels on the Bus," and "John Jacob Jingleheimer Schmidt," followed by twenty rounds of "Who Let The Dogs Out? (woof, woof, woof, woof, woof)"! Come to think of it, this might even be too torturous for YOU! Be strong and stick to the plan. You can deal with it. Your husband is weaker, and he'll break. Just wait till you approach the mic for your extensive performances every night. Those will truly be priceless!

77 Crown Yourself the Queen of Jealousy

Honestly, I've never been the jealous type, but boy, have I dealt with my share of wackadoo boyfriends whose pictures you will find under the definition of "jealous" in the dictionary. I always think there is always one jealous person in a relationship—and then there's the other partner, who becomes the object of control and obsession.

> **RISK INDICATOR: 1**
> *You're in the Clear*
> He'll be so relieved to find out you're not going crazy, he won't even care that you called his receptionist to set her skinny ass straight!

I strongly believe a healthy dose of jealousy is acceptable and somewhat necessary in the coupling world. Besides adding some spice to the union, jealousy provides a sense of competition, and makes the other person feel like a one-of-a-kind trophy, desperately desired and not easily replaced. We all like a little jealousy from time to time—and I have to admit I pretend to be jealous on occasion just so my husband thinks he's still "the man"; it keeps him happy, and it only requires a slight bit of effort on my part. I'll pout when he tells me he's having lunch with an attractive female business associate, or I'll suggest he has a crush on the new receptionist at his office. The truth is we've been married so long I could care less if he was going on an extended vacation to Manchuria with his receptionist, although I would be pretty upset if they didn't bring me back a souvenir.

See, men like it when we're a little jealous so they can complain to their "boys" about it and therefore make it seem like they're some hot commodity, but there's a fine line between a little jealous and "serial stalker," which is the line we're going to cross, hoping to send them into a state of complete fear and panic. If you are normally jealous, this will be easy-peasy. Just become a full-blown head case and demand to know where he is every second and who he's with, request his voice-mail password so you can listen to his messages, follow him around, listen in on his phone conversations, show up unexpectedly, and here's the clincher: videotape his whereabouts (a move that will surely send shivers down his shivers)! On the other hand, if you're not normally jealous, you'll have to start small, maybe by pointing out how you saw him eyeing your waitress during dinner, then work your way up to having a hissy fit when you catch him having an innocent chat with the female neighbor. Later on accuse him of having an affair, or even "wanting" to have an affair, for absolutely no reason. He'll be so confused he'll want to scream, but he'll think it's a phase and try to ignore it. You're not backing down, though, especially after figuring out his e-mail password and telling him you are monitoring his messages. Ransack his car during an "evidence search"; check all his pockets for phone numbers and suspicious business cards. Let him think you are completely demon-possessed, and just when he's ready to have a breakdown, go ahead and tell him you were just having a little fun at his expense. Although you do plan to keep that voice-mail password around . . . just in case.

78 Go Back to School

Do you really want to see a miserable husband? It's the guy whose wife has decided to go back to school to finally get that degree she's always wanted. The issue is not a husband trying to get in the way of his wife's dream. The real issue is a lazy, self-absorbed man suddenly being forced to deal with

RISK INDICATOR: 1
You're in the Clear
Let him rant and complain all he wants, but you should warn him it's not good for his ulcer.

his children and maybe even having to do some actual housework while his wife spends more time outside of the house. It is never too late to reach for your dream, and if your dream happens to be his nightmare, you are really on the right track.

Whether you are a stay-at-home mom or a working woman looking for a competitive edge, going back to school is never a waste of time, and even though it's a little scary, just think of the giant ulcer your husband will develop while you are expanding your horizons. That should help make your decision a little easier.

Research shows that the face of higher education is definitely changing. According to ABC News, nearly two million adults older than forty (60 percent of them women) are now enrolled in college looking to complete a degree, make a career change, or achieve professional advancement. So what does a typical husband do when his wife tells him she'd like to hit the books again and head back to school? Most likely, he does a lot of whining, pouting, and attempting to dissuade her. In all fairness, there are some men who would be truly supportive and do anything to help their wives through the transition, but I'm talking about a "typical man" who has grown accustomed to home-cooked meals and plenty of wifely pampering. This man will not be supportive, and will not stew in private either. He will do enough bellyaching and complaining for a family of five. I've seen it happen on at least two occasions. One of my dear girlfriends decided to go back to school after staying home for eight years caring for her two kids and her husband like a modern-day Cinderella. She did it all, the playgroups, the schlepping, the cooking, cleaning, shopping, doctor's appointments, homework, but all along, she had the burning desire to finish up a teaching degree she had grudgingly abandoned when she discovered she was pregnant just a year into her marriage. You would think her husband would have cheered her on like the best friend he's supposed to be. Oh no. He was so downright overwhelmed and dejected he begged her every day to forget about her goals and dreams and come back home so she could return to her old job of taking care of the kids (and everything else) full-time! His bad attitude only fueled her fire, and in the end she finally quenched that burning desire to wrap up her studies. She is now gainfully employed as an official teacher. Her husband still complains about the three years of hell he went through while she went back to school, but she knows it was all worth it.

79 Make Size Comparisons

Small, miniature, tiny, petite, infinitesimal, minuscule, teeny-weeny, itty-bitty, microscopic. All are words you should never use when you are referring to a man's package. "Cute" is also one of those special words—one that's completely acceptable when you are discussing a newborn baby or someone's pet dachshund, for example, but completely banished and frowned upon when it comes to extremely precarious

> **RISK INDICATOR: 4**
> *Watch Your Back*
> Here's the long and the "short" of it. Any man will be mentally scarred once you poke fun at his "fun zone." There's going to be some hell to pay, but it's entirely up to you to decide if it's worth it.

and highly personal penis discussions. Who would think such a seemingly innocuous entity would carry such ENORMOUS (pardon the pun) significance? To men, their entire world revolves around their penis. As the mother of a young boy, I can confidently say (with no studies or medical research required) that males become severely obsessed with their organs at around the age of six months, when they inadvertently grab hold of that thing and it suddenly becomes their new favorite toy.

Anyhow . . . later on, their deep penis fascination grows and eventually they discover that light fondling tends to feel quite good. Then they start rubbing up on your furniture, and it's all downhill from there! As we all know, penis obsession continues throughout a man's life, consuming his every thought, controlling his every action. That's why they do that incessant "penis handling" where they need to adjust it and just make sure "it's still there." Meanwhile, the largest component of penis obsession is SIZE.

According to American researchers Masters and Johnson (who basically did a whip-it out "schlong size survey"), 80 percent of men wish they had a bigger penis. (That is a heavy burden for one appendage if you ask me! It's kinda like wishing your arms were longer! And the worst part is there's *nothing* you can do about it!) With very good reason, men often express their fear that partners will silently judge and mentally measure them (which we do) and possibly leave them for a more "gifted" partner (which we often consider). Here are the results of the size survey: Out of 300 men, the largest male organ measured 5.5 inches in the flaccid state, and the smallest penis measured 2.25 inches (thankfully, I never dated that guy, but it belonged to a fairly heavily built man of 5'11"). It's also worth pointing out that there is no correlation between penile size and race. Now that you are armed

DON'T TRY THIS AT HOME!

Reuters, Moscow—
August 22, 2007

A woman set fire to her ex-husband's penis as he sat naked watching television and drinking vodka. Asked if the man would make a full recovery, a police spokeswoman said it was "difficult to predict." The attack climaxed three years of acrimonious enforced co-habitation. The couple divorced three years ago but continued to share a small flat, something common in Russia where property costs are very high. [I guess those savings didn't pay off in the end!]

with this information, you can have a frank and open conversation with your guy, making him feel as uncomfortable as sand in a butt crack. Discuss the fact that you would like to possibly do some measuring and see if he "falls short." You can also pick a really crucial time to engage in this discussion—like while you are both in the shower for instance (and he's suffering from inevitable shrinkage). I'll bet it will be one of those conversations he'll never forget, but wish he could!

80 Secretly Hire a Housekeeper

Doctors are sure housework won't kill you, but why take the risk? —AUTHOR UNKNOWN

> **RISK INDICATOR: 3**
> *He Might Be On to You*
> Houses don't magically clean themselves, so don't get too cocky and forget to cancel any cleaning services if you're ever away.

Most of us appreciate a spotless house. You know it the minute you walk through the door. That welcoming fresh scent fills your nostrils, a sure sign of immaculate counters, pristine floors, dust-free shelves, and sparkling bathrooms as sterile as an OR. Life is just easier when everything is clean and in its place, especially when you have children. Kids are mess magnets, and the younger the kid, the bigger the mess. Men can also be pretty darn sloppy and highly inconsiderate, leaving their crap always strewn about. I find my husband where his clothes trail ends. It usually starts with one of his serious "work ties" left abandoned in its noose-shaped form on the kitchen table; then you come across his white or blue dress shirt (he's very basic) crumpled on the floor just outside the bedroom door. Dress pants usually follow, thrown haphazardly on the bed, and next to that, his socks looking seemingly tired and deflated after a long day's work. I consider myself lucky when he spares me the revolting sight of his used underwear, which he tends to kindly leave right by the bathroom sink for me to deal with. This is why every wife can benefit from hiring a housekeeper for daily/ weekly visits, or employ a general cleaning lady on a freelance basis to help you periodically when you need an extra pair of hands. We all know a clean house is a thing of beauty, as long as someone else is doing it, so why do it at all? Outsourcing is a wonderful tool, and think of all the other stuff you can be doing while your house is being tidied up. You can spend more time with your kids or give yourself some time off to relax or go shopping all by yourself!

So the question is, Will your husband ever find out? Only if you really want him to.

The tips to not getting caught are 1) Always pay in cash. 2) Make sure your secret help is long gone before your hubby gets home. 3) Look a bit disheveled when he arrives and take credit for everything. In the end you'll be happy, and he'll always wonder how the house stays so sparkling clean! Remember, housework is as thankless as dieting; you work your ass off, only to find there's always more work to be done! Good for you for outsmarting him.

81 Refer to Yourself Only in the Third Person

Isn't this the most irritating bullshit on earth? Annoying people have been doing it for quite some time, but this "talking in third person" phenomenon has really gotten out of control since the dawn of that oh-so-special social networking site called "Facebook."

Now that Facebook has become a popular online medium, everyone has unfortunately been encouraged to share every insignificant minuscule detail of

RISK INDICATOR: 1
You're in the Clear
You aren't harming anyone here, just having some light-hearted fun. See how long you can keep the game going until you can't stand listening to yourself and go back to speaking like a human, not like a robot.

their dull, exceedingly ultra-normal lives. But here we are reading inane crap like "Heather just bought skinny jeans on sale!" or "Trevor is making sock puppets!"

Seriously, WHO CARES?? AND WHY DO WE PARTICIPATE IN THIS ENORMOUS TIME-SUCKING, BRAIN-DRAINING BASTION OF STUPIDITY? If people want to share so much of their all-important lives, they should just set up webcams on their foreheads! (And maybe we can all make some cash with advertising while we're at it!) But all this buildup is getting me to my point, my dear peeps. Because of Facebook, "online speak" has surreptitiously seeped into our every-day vocabulary and suddenly become the new "talking trend" or "hip lingo" (if you will). Now instead of just turning to your coworker and saying "You know, I feel like having a salad for lunch," you are now required to utter some edgy line like "Maria is going green for lunch and Sally is coming with!" Ugh!!

And ya know, if you feel the need to occasionally engage in this pathetic juvenile behavior, go on with your silly self, but I actually had a boss who spoke like this REGULARLY! He still has no clue how incredibly stupid people think he is. He would say things in meetings like "LARRY thinks that's a great idea!" or "Our department got another award because LARRY is da man!" Till this day "MARIA still wants to VOMIT when she remembers LARRY's pompous and idiotic behavior!"

Because this behavior is so unbelievably irritating, imagine dishing it out to your hubby consistently. He'll be so frustrated he'll want to tear every strand of his hair out (if he's not already bald, of course). In which case you could say "KAREN loves your new look, honey! She thinks you should have shaved your head years ago!" At first he might be a bit confused, but he'll catch on soon enough. If he calls you on it, just say "KAREN has no idea what you're talking about." Meanwhile . . . MARIA has to go now. It's been twelve minutes since I updated my Facebook profile.

PROOF POSITIVE

At the time of this publication, Facebook has more than 300 million active users. More than 6 billion minutes are spent on Facebook each day worldwide, with more than 40 million status updates posted daily. At least 24 million photos are uploaded every single day (most of which will be cropped or digitally altered if any females in them look fat or show any signs of thigh cellulite or premature aging!).

82 Suggest a Fabulous Staycation!

Who cares about traveling the world? There's so much to see and do right here at home (wherever that is), and it's a super-duper time to really bond with your family and get reacquainted with your spouse! (I feel like some phony cheerleader trying to sell you a crappy timeshare.) In all seriousness, though, deciding to stay home for

RISK INDICATOR: 1
You're in the Clear

He'll be just as pleased with all his hard work when he sees all the tasks he'll have accomplished. Keep the ibuprofen handy; he'll need it.

a vacation is no longer a travesty. You don't have to be embarrassed when you admit to friends and coworkers you've decided to keep it local and enjoy the not-so-finer things in your immediate surroundings. It's the "in thing" to do! Embrace it, enjoy it, and above all things, take advantage of it. How? Well, besides the priceless bonding and enriching local exploring (which is draining and overrated), staycations also offer heaps of free time to get to all of those at-home "projects" you've been putting off all year. Just start a list, and before you know it, you will have filled up every second of free time you thought you had so much of (especially your husband's!). You'll wonder, Why didn't we come up with this staycation stuff sooner? If you have children, you'll want to get them involved, too. They'll be "down with it," as long as you bribe them accordingly. You can also just promise to take them to delightfully dizzying Disney World, or whatever overpriced pee-infested local water park they'd like to visit during your time off. Just agree to their demands—whatever they are—so you can get to the business of tormenting your husband with backbreaking, painstaking chores.

So let's get to that list. Coming from someone who still has unpacked moving boxes from 1997, trust me, there is *always* work to be done in a home, no matter what the size.

And now that you have a partner around for at least seven to ten days to share the responsibility (whether he likes it or not), you can both jump in with gusto!

Start off with the larger, tougher tasks first (and hand those off to your hubby).

This includes anything that involves tools, painting, bulky items, climbing ladders, arduous landscaping, opening boxes, doing any sorting or rearranging, toxic chemicals, sharp items, or any type of machinery—especially but not exclusively a snowblower, leafblower, or power washer. Let's say your husband decides to stage a full-blown revolt, and refuses to comply with his work order. Take it in stride and go about your business. He'll come around when he sees what spending ten days with a cranky, frigid wife can do to a man. He'll be on the job after twenty-four hours. Which means he'll have to work even harder after wasting all that precious time! Getting him up bright and early is key. Rome wasn't built in a day, and that new gazebo for your garden isn't going up by itself, is it? Break time is over.

Chapter Five

MISCELLANEOUS TORTURE

83 *Rip Up His Lucky Shirt*

Don't even worry about the "bad juju." If the shirt were so damn lucky it wouldn't succumb to such a shitty fate, so go for it! Find it quick and get down to ripping for sheer pleasure. Lucky clothing usually hangs out smack-dab in the middle of a man's closet where he can always see it, rub it for good luck, and remember why it became his lucky shirt in the first place. It could be for a myriad of reasons, like he landed a great job wearing it, or got

> **RISK INDICATOR: 4**
> *Watch Your Back*
> Hopefully you will not be haunted by "the sprit of the lucky shirt" and you'll continue living a charmed life. Good ol' karma has a way of catching up to all of us, though, so keep your guard up and buy a lucky bamboo tree just in case.

some action with the hottest chick alive, or he won some crucial game . . . but who cares, really? It won't be his lucky shirt for long because it will soon be gone, gone, gone! If your husband happens to fall under the highly superstitious category, and possesses a talisman of good fortune (like a lucky shirt), doing away with it will really make him come undone.

Personally, I always start with the buttons. Plucking them off one by one, letting the silly shirt know its final moments are near. Then I take scissors and slowly loosen the sleeve seams . . . reveling in the unraveling thread. Finally, his lucky shirt is ready for its unluckiest moment. Hold the sleeves simultaneously and give 'em the tug of your life! The second you hear the material tearing apart you'll feel instant release and gratification, as if a dark spell has been broken.

Next, move on to the collar. Use the scissors to slice it up . . . do it all over, and yank that insidious rag apart till your biceps burn. The irony is that it may be days, weeks, months, or even years before your guy notices his lucky shirt is missing. In the end you'll be doing a him a great service. After all, superstitions are for losers. Real winners fix the game.

PROOF POSITIVE

The Urban Dictionary (yes, there is one) defines "bad juju" as "being haunted by a bad vibe or aura." And just in case you're wondering . . . it can be used as a noun or an adjective. "I juju, you juju, everybody juju!"

84 Send a Strip-O-Gram

Don't you worry, sistah, I am one step ahead of you. OF COURSE I wouldn't send a hot and sexy FEMALE stripper for my husband to enjoy! Instead, send a MALE stripper to his office and sit back to savor the hilarity that will no doubt ensue. This torture exercise is a major no-brainer, yet it doesn't immediately pop into our minds

RISK INDICATOR: 2
Caution, Girlfriend
Overall good judgment is required here. Only you know your husband's work environment, and can decide whether the prank will be well-received or score your hubby a one-way ticket to the unemployment line.

when we think of pulling a prank on our guys because male strippers are usually reserved for "chick events" like birthday parties or bachelorette bashes. But now we know better, right? It's absolute genius, and all it takes is a delightful phone call or e-mail if you'd like to avoid a possible awkward personal discussion. (I actually did this once to a cheating boyfriend, and the woman on the other end of the phone not only laughed her derrière off, she congratulated me on such a phenomenal scheme!) You could ambush your man at the office on any given workday just for laughs OR you could wait for a special event like an anniversary or birthday to move in for the kill and give him the shock of his life! He'll probably hide under his desk for the duration of it, or run for cover, but it's a complete blast no matter what happens in the end!

Here's how the plan should go down: Ask around for possible references in your search for a quality strip company. Yes, I know it sounds like an oxymoron, but some of these businesses have been around a lot longer than others, employ a better staff, and the "performers" take their craft very seriously. Take it from me, the choices can be overwhelming, with many different services offered (as well as lengthy price list) so you'll want to choose carefully. Remember, it's all about complete customer "satisfaction" (ahem) . . . and ultimately, you want the best your money can buy. So put it out there—maybe one of your girlfriends has used a great place before, and she might have the name and number handy! After you've found the right place, ideally you'll be able to go online and see the "goods" for yourself. Most reputable strip companies post pictures of their performers (as well as a list of their specialties such as "great dancer," "double-jointed," or "freakishly endowed") to help you choose the right one for the occasion. A word of caution here—as you know, things online are not always as they appear (especially when it comes to height), so if the guy's measurements aren't listed and you are looking for the perfect full-size heartthrob to do the job, call up and ask. Either way, once you make a choice, pay the costs, and set the date, you are ready for some true excitement. You might want to get your husband's assistant and any female coworkers in on the prank (if you are sure no one will blow the whistle!). This will be a trick on your husband, but a definite treat for any ladies who will be around to witness the spectacle. When you get the phone call, your husband will either be raging mad or laughing uncontrollably. Hopefully it will be the latter, but if it's not, you can always deny. Just say you meant to send a fruit basket and they got their bananas mixed up!

85 Shop 'til He Drops

Besides treating yourself to an impromptu shopping spree and spending every penny in your joint bank and money-market accounts, the next best thing you can do to inflict severe torture on your man is to actually TAKE HIM WITH YOU when you hit the mall and spend every penny you both

> **RISK INDICATOR: 1**
> *You're in the Clear*
> Once you get him to the mall, he might secretly wish he had never met you, but other than bore him to tears you've really done nothing wrong. You should feel more guilt after indulging in that sinful Cinnabon at the food court.

own. Approach this exercise as Olympian Michael Phelps would, and just go for all the gold ever made! This is your best sport, after all. Women *invented* this sport, and on your shopping day you will be the best in the entire stratosphere! Titleholder, world champion shopper extraordinaire!

I actually know some men who don't mind shopping, but they enjoy it only for so long. An hour, maybe two—or even three if it involves a stop for a greasy Philly cheesesteak. But keep in mind we're talking MARATHON SHOPPING for this special occasion; the kind you hit the gym two weeks before to engage in. You must be ready, properly dressed, agile, hydrated. He should be the exact opposite: caught off-guard, wearing uncomfortable footwear, tired, thirsty, and hungry. This is best done during a "holiday sale" of any type. You name it . . . Christmas sale, AFTER Christmas sale, New Year's bargain hunting, Memorial Day blowouts, Fourth of July sizzling offers, and massive Labor Day clearances! Anytime the malls are packed to capacity and parking is guaranteed to be hellish will be the ideal situation. Making him miss a an all-important football game on TV would be sublime, and bringing your kids along would truly be the topping on our deliciously devilish cake.

Even thinking about this shopping scenario would make any man shudder, so just consider the massive torture that awaits. Here are some special tips to bear in mind:

- Stop at every store, even if you don't need anything there! "Oh, it's the Boxes Galore Store! Let's check it out!" How many times have you forced your husband to browse around Restoration Hardware (which SOUNDS like an upscale Home Depot, but is really a Pottery Barn in disguise!). Men absolutely LOATHE this store because most of the stuff in it is purely decorative, and, in his opinion, generally useless, which will infuriate him further.

- Make him hold your purse. After all, you need both hands to tackle those giant clothes racks (which tend to be tightly overfilled). Men feel like giant buffoons when they are forced to carry our bags because not only do they look ridiculous, everyone brands them as "whipped" and seriously controlled by their women.

- Don't just go with a "visual" approval. Try everything on and demand his opinion. Is the color right for you? Should you get a bigger or smaller size? Can this transition from daywear to nightwear? Would this go better with heels or flats?

- Don't be selfish and just shop for yourself. Be sure to select various outfits for your hubby to try on too! You know how they adore feeling exposed in a dressing room, and judged upon their emergence from it. (Yes, I'm being sarcastic.) Also, keep him in the dressing room as long as possible by handing him extra outfits to try on while he's changing. He'll have no choice but to cooperate.

- If he throws a tantrum at any point, add fifteen minutes of extra mall time to your journey. If he wants to act like a toddler, he will be treated as one.

- Once you are done at one mall, there's always another one the next town over.

Engage in a "mall tour" if you so desire. You can easily do two or three in a day depending on your stamina. Just don't let him do the driving, 'cause he'll head home before you can say "Urban Outfitters."

PROOF POSITIVE

According to the World Almanac, the Mall of America, located in Bloomington, Minnesota, is considered to be the largest super-mall in the United States when it comes to overall size and floor area, but because the mall has less retail space than Philadelphia's King of Prussia Mall, it actually ranks as number two on the list of the largest retail facilities in America. Either way, getting to either one is the goal, and a dream come true for any shopping addict!

86 Circulate His Most Embarrassing Pictures

Picture this: A not-so-pleasantly-plump eight-year-old girl hysterically crying because she just wet her denim rainbow pants in a McDonald's parking lot, and her sister is gleefully pointing out the large stain to the camera, capturing this delightfully embarrassing

RISK INDICATOR: 2
Caution, Girlfriend

Unleashing an embarrassing picture campaign could bring waves of laughter, but a vengeful deluge could be on the horizon should your own embarrassing photos surface. Watch your ass and make sure it's covered if there happens to be a camera in close proximity.

memory on film for eons to come. (Thanks, Mom, for having that flash ready!) That, my friends, is my most embarrassing picture EVER, and it continues to haunt me . . . passed around by my endless array of family members who still can't get enough of it till this very day! (In my defense, we were on a lengthy road trip, I had one too many Slurpees, and I REALLY had to go. But my parents chose to ignore my endless pleas to potty and kept on driving, which led to the soggy and ultra-humiliating outcome.)

Most people have an embarrassing picture they wish would have never been taken. For some reason, men are especially embarrassed by innocuous photographs, like the naked ones their moms took of them when they were babies. Maybe it's because their "giblets" look really tiny and they fear judgment, but in any case, there's just something about a nude baby photo that makes a man want to scream. Usually any photos from a boy's prepubescent period can bring on mammoth doses of anxiety—you know, before they were "Masters of the Universe," when their moms still dressed them, and when they didn't have a manly reputation to protect. Anyhow, you can always get your hands on some shocking shots, and for distribution all you need is your handy-dandy computer. Yep, scan those puppies in if you have to, put together a colorful arrangement of pics, pull up your e-mail address book, and just press send! Your friends will all get a good laugh, and if you want to let your hubby in on the joke, include him in the mass e-mail.

Encourage others to distribute at will, and we're really talking mass mailing here. It's all about going "viral" these days, right?

So start looking through those old albums, or maybe there's a recent laughter-worthy pic of your guy just waiting to be shared and enjoyed for centuries to come.

87 *Post His Sports Memorabilia on Ebay*

My man is seriously obsessed with his balls and his bat. Sure, we could be talking about his nether region . . . but we're not. Nope, his prized possessions are a slew of baseballs signed by famous sluggers, a Dolphins football autographed by hottie ex-quarterback Dan Marino, and a bat signed by Hall of Famer Reggie Jackson. He's also got a behemoth collection of baseball cards, a Cowboys football hel-

> **RISK INDICATOR: 5**
> *Run Like Hell*
> If you play your cards right—so to speak—you should get away with selling a couple of not-so-obvious items from your hubby's sports stash. If and when he finds out, hit the road and don't look back!

met signed by Zach Thomas, a Fortieth Anniversary plaque featuring actual infield dirt from Shea Stadium, zillions of collector's items, and a water bottle he swears was chugged on by Peyton Manning. My husband started his sports memorabilia collection since before he had chest hair. You can imagine what this stuff means to him. To me they are all just major dust collectors (which are a bitch to clean), but to him they are his pride and joy, his babies, his lifelong work. It takes true effort and dedication to amass such a collection (and having a whole other house would be nice 'cause we are busting at the seams storing all his junk over here!). In fact, if "memorabilia collecting" itself could be considered a sport, my husband would be the MVP every year. As you know, the sports memorabilia world is complicated and cutthroat. Selling sports memorabilia is a billion-dollar industry in the United States, and the bigger the sports name, the bigger the return.

There's no doubt authentic sports items can fetch some nice coin, and that's precisely why we're discussing my hubby's and your hubby's collections. Even though most precious sports-related memorabilia fetches major bucks, we don't have time to deal with Sotheby's in New York or Field of Dreams (the ultimate sports gift store). We want to move quickly and quietly using the most attainable medium around.

We're talking eBay, baby! The online auction source. The mother lode! Yes, this is where we want to be. Now remember, though, since torture is our main motivator, the actual cash we attain isn't what's important. After all the painstaking care men take to collect their sports junk, selling it off for little or almost nothing would be the worst punishment imaginable! Proudly display the items and hope for the best. Craigslist is also an excellent selling source, just in case you're taking notes . . . although I've had wonderfully delightful exchanges on eBay. Did I just admit that? Oh well, it's not like my husband even knows what's missing from his collection. That's what happens when you have so much junk that you forget what you actually have. Which makes it so much easier to sell . . .

88 *Finally Open Up to His Family*

Go ahead and tell your husband's oh-so-perfect mother how her cooking really sucks, show his dear old grandmother that naughty butt tattoo you've been covering up for years, or maybe come clean about the time you and your husband hooked up in the laundry room during a holiday visit. Anytime is the ideal time to let it all hang out and drive your hubby to the brink. In fact, you can start your very own "Shock and Awe" campaign. Telling the truth and getting wild reactions

> **RISK INDICATOR: 4**
> *Watch Your Back*
> Coming clean is a wonderful feeling and will no doubt upset your man, but it does have its drawbacks, especially if someone decides to read you the riot act at the next family gathering. Just know it's a double-edged sword that at times could be sharper than you'd like.

can be quite addictive. (You might find yourself enjoying it too much and you might have to put the brakes on eventually, but oh what fun you will have in the meantime.) How about telling his dad what an absolute cheapskate you really think he is? Maybe it's time everyone knows how Cousin Harry likes to grab your thigh when no one's looking, or how Uncle Rob constantly gives you "bedroom eyes" across the dinner table. Sordid family secrets are meant to be shared, so let's get into the sharing mood! Aren't you sick and tired of playing it safe? Always saying the right thing or walking away from a confrontation rather than embracing it? We've all been in a position when we're spending time with our in-laws (and possibly their wacky extended family) and we wish we could disclose what's really going on in our heads, but instead we stuff it down in the name of peace. Why do we torture ourselves? You won't believe how freeing it can be to unleash those thoughts and purge your poor repressed soul!

I finally had it one day with a certain relative whose breath was so downright offensive it could not only choke a horse, but kill every human and animal within a fifty-mile radius! Forget anthrax or germ warfare! This particular case of halitosis (if somehow bottled) could be used by terrorists to obliterate entire cities or villages! Anyhow, after years of dealing with this nuisance (and downing an entire bottle of Manischewitz wine), I decided to take a stand and finally said, "HAVE YOU ANY IDEA HOW FRIGGIN' NASTY YOUR BREATH IS?"

I didn't mean to blurt it out in such a cruel manner. There's just something about being a bit tipsy that makes you talk extra loud, and I kinda got out of control, but I just had to say it once and for all! A couple of other family members noticed, I heard only crickets for a bit, and then the victim of my tirade sheepishly excused himself/herself. We haven't spoken much since then, but I'm still hoping that moment was life-changing for the better. (Who knows? Maybe he/she got some medical attention or at the very least started carrying around some Altoids.) Either way, by opening up I freed myself of those repressed emotions, and my husband was mortified in the process. So get with it. Make no apologies. Take no prisoners. No one is safe. Be brutally honest when everyone least expects it. Think of it as freeing therapy— and you don't even have to pay for it!

89 *Kidnap His PDA*

My husband is hopelessly in love . . . with his BlackBerry. They met about five years ago, and have been inseparable ever since. His trusty electronic mate provides all the things my dear hubby craves—constant companionship and complete, unconditional devotion. "SHE" is always there (at hand's reach) to offer crucial information in an absolute flash. Never cranky or unavailable (like me, for example).

> **RISK INDICATOR: 5**
> *Run Like Hell*
> You have no idea what coming between him and his "special lady" can do to your Man, and keep in mind it could adversely affect his job. Hope for the best, but prepare for the worst.

Always organized, always ready to give her all. And boy, does she deliver. Phone calls, e-mail, text messages, necessary reminders, urgent notices, and she even wakes up my husband from his slumber with a cheery ring each morning. (I can see why she's better than a REAL wife, right?) This is why I've nicknamed her his CrackBerry; it's because of his serious and troubling addiction. He cannot go an entire three minutes without making contact with this piece of technological ass. After all, they share so much—juicy secrets, private jokes, and plans I may never know about. It's a romance to last through the ages. Complete, all-consuming devotion.

Admittedly, I am envious of this highly co-dependent, impervious relationship. After all, how can I, made of flesh and blood, compete with a device such as this? She never gets tired of being probed and groped, she's never frustrated with her relationship or makes annoying demands. No, she doesn't have dreams or requests, nor does she provide any disappointments. She just needs to be charged. So it's official. THAT BITCH HAS GOT TO GO!

While your husband is sleeping (since that's virtually the only time he's not attached at the hip to the damn thing), steal his beloved gadget, turn off the ringer, and hide that sucker in the bottom of the hamper. Your guy will wake up in a cold sweat (that is, if he's able to wake up without his electronic lover signaling it's 6 A.M.), and as you feign sympathy at his plight, you can secretly gloat at your ingenious trick! Let him sweat for as long as you'd like to continue the torture, and then emerge the hero on laundry day. You might even get a nice dinner out of it!

90 Make Sure His Best Suit Never Makes It to the Cleaners

You know the feeling when you're headed out with the girls, all ready to wear your favorite sheer blouse and the pair of Calvins that make your bottom look like a perfectly ripe apple, only to find within fifteen minutes of needing to leave that both are hopelessly wrinkled and dirty and in the

> **RISK INDICATOR: 3**
> *He Might Be On to You*
> Playing dumb will only work if you can keep a straight face and find a killer hiding spot for the wrinkly suit. Either way, he definitely won't let you near the darn thing again.

bottom of the laundry pile? Or even worse, stuck at the dry cleaners, which inconveniently closed two hours earlier? I don't know about you, but for me, supreme disappointment sets in when I have to settle for the second-best outfit, especially when I was envisioning myself confidently strutting my stuff in more stylish duds.

Well, believe me, your man is likely just as concerned with how he looks before that power lunch or important client meeting, and that's why you can inflict some serious torture by messing with his favorite suit. Wait until it's soiled (or very wrinkled) and kindly offer to take care of it so he doesn't have to deal with the dry cleaning. Your man will trust that you are handling the situation (after all, he leaves ALL the tedious laundry sorting and folding and dry-cleaning schlepping to you, right?). You then proceed to do a few things. Conveniently "forget" to drop it off with the rest of the delicates and claim amnesia when he asks about it week after week. ("What suit? I don't remember that one.") Your husband will go berserk and might even end up shelling out for another one. To prevent him from breaking out the plastic on goodies for himself (I mean, his hard-earned money should be spent on jewelry for you!), let the game go on for a week or so, and then either magically produce the suit, or slip the suit back into the closet. Act as if it had been there all along. Your husband will surely think he's going crazy.

91 *Destroy His Recliner*

Is there anything more appropriately named than a La-Z-Boy? The name itself describes exactly what women have been thinking since the dawn of time. Men are the laziest slobs in the stratosphere, so what a harmonious union a lazy man and his La-Z-Boy make! Few things bring a man more joy than a cushy chair nestling his backside ever so gently, caressing every contour of his body with its cozy, warm good-

RISK INDICATOR: 5
Run Like Hell

C'mon, you know you're playing with fire. If you take the dark path and ruin his upholstered best friend, a heavy fine you must pay. When he discovers his wet, torched, or ripped buddy, make sure your running shoes are on.

ness. He need not request a date with his recliner, he need not beg for a tender embrace when he's feeling down, nor hear its complaints after a tough day. His recliner is always there; quiet, patient, welcoming. He desperately longs for its luxuriously upholstered essence. His unwavering friend awaits to wash away his stress, lessen his pain, or bestow the simple pleasure of providing the ideal setting for a delicious afternoon snooze.

Personally, I think the well-intended folks at La-Z-Boy literally went off their rockers when the "E-cliner" was introduced, featuring built-in WebTV Internet access and tools.

(I mean honestly, why leave the house anymore?) But over the years so much thought has gone into making man's La-Z-Boy dreams a reality, it is now a challenge to destroy it appropriately. My advice? Spend a good chunk of time considering your destructive options.

Knife mutilation? Torching? Acid burning? All wonderfully creative and incredibly enjoyable chair-destroying options. Still, I highly recommend the simple yet extremely effective leaving-it-out-in-the-pouring-rain approach. Or let your crazy messy kids go to town! Talk about easy! Anyone with kids (no matter their age, size, or fitness level) knows the damage they can cause to furniture. Kids should actually be used in factory testing. I assure you it would sound like this: "Yes sir, the sofa made it through all of the durability tests, but miserably failed to hold up in the toddler room." As far as kids are concerned, toddlers are specially skilled in the art of sofa destruction. It would take only one day to do irreparable damage. Just give a toddler full access to food and office supplies, and that should do the trick. Think of the havoc that kid could achieve with just some Oreo cookies and your average Sharpie, scissors, or a fresh tube of Super Glue; enough damage to make your sofa-obsessed man want to buy the farm. That is, until he falls in love with his next recliner (featuring a retractable toilet and ESPN instant-replay button).

92 *Prove Him Wrong*

Have you ever gotten into a heated discussion with a bull-headed man? No matter how stupid he sounds or how factually incorrect he may be, he will stick to his guns and claim you are wrong, just because he refuses to

RISK INDICATOR: 2
Caution, Girlfriend
We all make stupid claims or comments from time to time. Be ready to take it from your man, if you plan on dishing it out.

admit defeat. I'll tell you about one of my encounters with such a man. Let's call this man Greg. He's actually a couple screws short of a toolbox, but thinks he's right up there with Einstein. Well, Greg used to be my neighbor, and somehow during an afternoon of grilling and neighborly socializing we got into a heated discussion about . . . tornadoes. Yep, tornadoes.

I'm not sure what possessed him at the time—maybe it was the pitcher of margaritas he had guzzled—but completely demented Greg was actually arguing that tornadoes come UP from under the ground, like they were trapped gas or something! Now seriously, what do you do in a situation like this? My five-year-old knows tornadoes don't come up from under the ground, but here's a forty-year-old making such a ludicrous statement! At first I was patient and respectful, politely informing dear Greg that he wasn't entirely correct (honestly, he was more off-mark than Dick Cheney was in that unfortunate hunting incident), but I didn't want to offend or humiliate him. I was just concerned that he actually believed that he was right and could risk embarrassing himself further. I was nice and said, "I'm sorry Greg, but you are mistaken. I'm no card-carrying scientist, but tornadoes happen when two masses of air—one warm, one cool—collide and form a funnel cloud. Trust me, I studied them closely in college, and even considered going on a tornado-chasing expedition one summer." His response? "Girlie, you have no idea what you're talking about!" I didn't get mad. I got factual. Not only did I break out the *National Geographic* tornado videos I own, but I went online and printed a bunch of articles on what make tornadoes tick. Needless to say, Greg finally had to admit I was right. I did the dignified thing of course . . . and proceeded to gloat like a child while doing the "cabbage patch end-zone victory dance." (I know, but it felt good to finally shut him up and get him to admit he was ridiculously wrong!) Meanwhile, Greg didn't take his loss too well, and refused to engage in any major discussions with me again. But my encounter illustrates just how far the male ego will go—so far as to risk complete embarrassment at the hands of a smarter woman. So the next time your man makes some ridiculous statement and refuses to admit he's not the brightest crayon in the box, make sure to drudge up FACTUAL evidence to prove the monosynaptic cretin absolutely positively wrong.

93 *Make Him an Offer He Can't Refuse*

So we're talking blackmail here. You got a problem wit dat? Call for a formal "Sopranos-style" sit-down, order large amounts of sausage, pasta, and red wine, and get right down to discussing any important personal family business. Hey, if it works for the mob, it will work for you. Threaten, coerce, and pressure your hubby to do whatever you desire, and make him understand that

> **RISK INDICATOR: 4**
> *Watch Your Back*
> Sometimes you gotta play dirty to get a job done. Just stay on your toes. (And if your name is "Apollonia," don't take any driving lessons from anyone named Michael.)

disappointing you would make him a big *stunad* (Italian for moronic idiot) and he should do everything in his power to make you happy.

Let's say you want a certain new car, an updated state-of-the-art kitchen, a lavish getaway, some new flashy jewelry, a pricey designer bag, or that gorgeous new coat you've been eyeing at Bergdorf's. Tell him he should "do the right thing" and make it happen—OR ELSE. And don't get bogged down with the details. It is definitely better if you let his imagination take over. Women can be very intense and mysterious when we want to be . . . so become Don Corleone's dedicated understudy and work your magic. *Capice?*

Family comes first, of course, so if it's something you'd like to acquire for the kids (like a million-dollar in-ground pool, a new gigantic outdoor play set, or something like a grand piano for your little prince or princess to practice on), ask nicely, and if he turns you down, that's when you turn up the heat and say something like, "You wouldn't want to bring shame to the family, would you?" He'll wonder where you're coming from, but will surely be too terrified or perplexed to challenge you.

When it comes to a personal favor, well, we all understand how one hand washes the other, so when you make a request, let your husband know it will be in his "best interest" to comply. For example, consider this scenario: you and one of your siblings want to open a business, you need a considerable amount of moola to make it happen, and most likely your hubby won't be too approving of the situation (if you know what I mean). You fully expect him to turn down the proposition and refuse to cooperate. He might say he's protecting his interests, but in traditional "Godfatherspeak," you will patiently and confidently say, "Sweetie, your interests are fine, as long as they don't conflict with mine." A savvy and highly intelligent "Don" (i.e., head of the family) would never give someone a chance to say no; rather, he would make his associate see the positive in this new business venture (like keeping full use of his legs, for example) and allow said associate to change his mind. When you put things in a certain perspective, it is truly amazing how people start seeing things your way.

So raise a glass and celebrate your newfound mutually beneficial relationship. This agreement is sure to be the start of something good. Enjoy some tasty antipasto and wash it down with chilled limoncello (mind-blowing Italian lemon-flavored liqueur).

Badda bing, badda bang, badda boop, everyone's happy!

94 *Purposely Ruin His Laundry*

Marriage is about the most expensive way for the average man to get laundry done.—BURT REYNOLDS

My husband and I have a euphemism for sex. Since our son came along we've taken to calling it "doing the laundry." To be honest with you, I think our quite

> **RISK INDICATOR: 1**
> *You're in the Clear*
> Chalk it up to a big boo-boo!
> He'll just have to take your word for it!

astute five-year-old has already figured it out (and thinks his parents are a couple of clowns), but nevertheless, if and when the subject of

"S-E-X" comes up, we immediately begin discussing "rinse cycles" and whether or not we've been using the right "fabric softener."

Conversely, when the topic of actual laundry comes up, the conversation is very scarce. There is no witty exchange, no coy laughter, no secret midnight appointments to do necessary "sorting" or "folding." The only thing you hear is the front door closing as my husband makes a speedy exit. Laundry is as foreign to my husband as dentists are to the British. What's worse is that he actually has the *cojones* to complain should his clothes not turn out exactly as desired. I always tell him, laundry machines have a mind of their own, and once something goes in you never know how it will come out. You're lucky if the emerging article of clothing bears even a remote resemblance to its original design—and that's not even when we're actively trying to ruin anything! With that said, the pickier the husband, the better the resulting reaction will be.

So what can you do to purposely ruin laundry, you ask? Well, for starters, you've probably inadvertently whipped up your very own "tie-dyed" batch of laundry where something bleeds, and the color runs into everything (most likely staining those ultra-expensive slacks you just purchased two days ago), and that's when you learned to always read clothing labels before a wash. Well, that's an idea right there! Sort clothes into "his" and "hers" piles and go to town on HIS favorite items. Throwing in a red sock, an unwanted lipstick, and even a kid's crayon or marker will do wonders. (Pink, preferably, to add insult to injury.) You can say it was just a mistake, you left your lipstick inside a pocket . . .

Here's another terrific way to do some major laundry sabotage: Shrink it till it can't shrink no more! My husband is always complaining that I've "shrunk" his clothing. (He may be right, but I always attribute it to his growing, protruding belly.) Anyhow, shrinking clothing is a great form of torture, because the clothes aren't completely ruined, but they could be pretty much unwearable. Shrinking is incredibly simple. Just crank your dryer to ninety minutes and repeat for about four hours. When his clothes come out he'll be lucky if they even fit your cat! And finally, if ruining his laundry is the goal, just read the instruction label and do everything it says not to do (this works perfectly with those items marked "dry clean only"). If all else fails, there's always good old bleach.

But all this fun does not come without repercussions. Do you recall when your hubby said he would give you the shirt off his back? Yeah, well, those days are over, but the last laugh will be yours.

PROOF POSITIVE

According to the Soap and Detergent Association (there's actually an association for this!), the average American family does more than 600 thousand loads of laundry per year, with women doing 88 percent of those loads. (No surprise there.)

95 Go to Town on his Golf Clubs

This section is intended to make Tiger Woods and every other golf-obsessed wackadoo (your hubby included) quiver in their God-awful golf shoes. For the record, I know that droves of women are totally into golf and take the game seriously. (I made the mistake during my radio show one

RISK INDICATOR: 5
Run Like Hell
Once he sees what you've done, you'll be lucky if he doesn't club you with one of his clubs!

day of saying "most women hate golf," and boy, did I pay dearly for my casual comment. The phones lit up like a Christmas tree with irate female callers!) Okay, so golf is not JUST a man's game, but I guess since those of us who aren't into it are subjected to our husbands' Tiger worship on a regular basis, we can safely deduce that the sport is saturated by testosterone. So if your man is madly consumed with golf and actually plays the game, messing with his golf equipment will no doubt torture his soul and inflict emotional pain or distress, which is exactly what we're "putting" for (that's a little golf humor for you)!

The plan of execution can involve several scenarios, but the target will be the same: his golf clubs. Golf freaks tend to spend a ridiculous amount of time worshipping, cleaning, and shining their equipment. As a perfect punishment, you'll want to do the exact opposite. Go nuts and muddy them, scratch them, and deface them in any way you see fit. If you're feeling especially impassioned, take your aggression out on his clubs by banging them with a hammer, or by leaving his designer golf bag outside during a downpour. If you know your guy can't afford to replace his clubs, you can still dole out some mighty devious tricks. Try pouring sticky rubber cement all over the grips, or pulling his putter and driver out of the bag before a big tournament! As far as his balls are concerned . . . well, I think you can be quite creative when it comes to those, so I'll leave that entirely up to you! (Insert wild, evil laughter.) Obviously, you'll have to pull this off when he's not around, and when you have a good amount of time on your hands to fully enjoy the experience. Believe me, stress relief like this is hard to find. Definitely a hole in one.

PROOF POSITIVE

Gallup Poll results show that among fans of professional golf, just over half (51 percent) say they are more likely to watch a golf tournament on TV if they know Tiger Woods will be playing! I am with the 49 percent of the population who would rather be watching paint dry or taking a long leisurely nap, uninterrupted by the sounds of any sporting event in the background.

96 *Make Him Late for Work (and Everything Else!)*

Being late sucks. Especially if you miss something really good like free money, or a bride falling on her face as she enters her wedding. Women are notoriously accused of making men run late because we take an inordinate amount of time getting dressed, doing our hair, getting makeup on, or even choosing our outfit in the first place, because we think

RISK INDICATOR: 3
He Might Be On to You
Don't overdo it—after all, you don't want him to *lose* his job. Getting him majorly peeved and making him tardy is the overall goal. If you achieve that, consider it a mission accomplished.

everything makes us look like Ms. Piggy. I'll be the first to admit that this does happen from time to time, but for the most part, I'm pretty punctual. I have to be, because I married "Mr. Right on Time." Andrew was even early to his own birth. He actually wheeled his mother into the delivery room! I suspect he'll be early for his own funeral too, greeting folks at the door while the formaldehyde is still setting in.

I think men hate being late because they think it's a negative reflection of their character. They feel it makes them look irresponsible and absent-minded. Women, on the other hand, think being late is a God-given right. If you want us to look good, you have to deal with the consequences!

If you happen to share your life with an early bird, you know how easily they come undone when they are pressed for time, so it's your mission to press further and watch them explode. Being on time for work of course is a top priority for our men, so play these dirty little tricks whenever you need a good laugh: Switch his alarm (and any backups) from AM to PM. He will freak out and it will throw off his entire day! If he showers before you, beat him to the tub and take an extra-long time scrubbing up. Hide his deodorant. Criticize his attire by asking him questions like, "You're gonna wear that?" or, "Is it Slob Day at your office?" He'll take forever to choose a more appropriate outfit. Another simple "late to work trick" is to get rid of his keys. Drop 'em behind the couch, or slide them under the bed. Again, always blame the kids when you can, or pets if you have them. If your husband has breakfast at home before he's off, burn his toast, "inadvertently" drop jelly on his crisp clean shirt, or spill a glass of coffee or orange juice all over his suit. You can also feign illness and ask him to take the kids to school at the last minute (they really hate that). Get in his way whenever you can. If you pack him a lunch, do it at the last minute, start an argument, misplace important files, drop his cell phone in the sink. He'll be a raving lunatic by the time he actually reaches the office . . . hopefully before lunchtime.

97 Create a Hubby Voodoo Doll

Wouldn't it be great if you could realistically put an evil curse on someone? I'll tell you, I would be unstoppable! There wouldn't be a man left standing! I jest, of course, but you can make your black magic dreams come true (in a less menac-

> **RISK INDICATOR: 4**
> *Watch Your Back*
> Messing with the occult always has its drawbacks . . . especially when your man can craft his own doll with your old duds. Misplaced any old T-shirts lately?

ing way) by crafting your very own husband voodoo doll—and at least *pretend* you could actually control his mind and body! So to help you understand the mysterious art of voodoo better, let's journey down the road of discovery together, shall we?

According to the *Columbia Encyclopedia*, voodoo is a native West African religious belief introduced to the New World by slaves. Voodoo believers are vastly numerous in Haiti, where voodoo was granted official religious status in 2003 (good to know!). Now here's the scoop: voodoo contends that all of nature is controlled by spiritual forces that must be acknowledged and honored through offerings and animal sacrifice. Ecstatic trances (a means of communicating with the gods and spirits) and magical practices play an important role in its ritual.

Armed with this newly acquired knowledge, we can proceed with our creepy-cool, neato-mosquito, voodoo-doll–making process! During my deep, intense, and insightful research, which included a visit to a spell store in lower Manhattan, I learned that voodoo dolls can be made from all kinds of stuff like paper, yarn, clay, cornhusks, candle wax, sponges, socks, potatoes, and discarded roof insulation (provided you can stand the massive itching from the fiberglass). But according to my "magical sources," the best material you could use for the "perfect" voodoo doll is actually a piece of cloth belonging to your intended "victim" (for lack of a better word). Getting ahold of a shred of your hubby's clothing should be a pretty simple task. Kidnapping one of his old tattered T-shirts is probably your best bet because he most likely won't miss it. Take the piece of square cloth, stuff some cotton into the middle, and use a simple rubber band to fashion a "head." Make sure to give it eyes, nose, and a mouth for effect. Another juicy voodoo tidbit is to make your doll as authentic as possible, by using hair from your hubby's brush for example, to really add a personal touch. All right, done. Now here comes the fun part. What to do once you've created your perfect mini-man? Hmm . . . the options are endless. You are in complete control. Use pushpins to inflict imaginary pain, let the dog use it as a chew toy, go online and discover all kinds of wacky spells you can cast, bind it, burn it, anything goes! Yell at the damn thing if it makes you feel better! The convenient thing about voodoo dolls is that they don't answer back or give you attitude. They are yours to torture any way your little heart desires. Leaving the doll lying around is also an ideal torture method. He'll be so terrified to ask what it is he'll just pray for divine intervention.

98 Venture Out to Vegas

Sorry, boys. This is a testosterone-free getaway.

Book it first-class all the way, baby! Round up the ladies, score a flight, and set your sights on sensational Sin City. Your husband will be tortured the minute you book your flight! Plan on gambling yourself giddy, shopping till your

> **RISK INDICATOR: 3**
> *He Might Be On to You*
> After you party like a rock star, your husband will be on the hunt for any "incriminating" evidence (pics, receipts, newly acquired wedding rings, things of that nature). Tattoos, however, will be more difficult to conceal, so skip 'em altogether.

arms ache, eating and drinking yourself to blissful oblivion, and as far as possible "encounters," well, you know the old saying: What happens in Vegas stays in Vegas! (But we will hunt down any and all witnesses AND their next of kin should they even attempt to recall any sordid details of your stay.) That last part was added for effect, of course, but you get the picture! For those who have never made a jaunt to the "jewel in the desert," know that Vegas is not for wimps. You should be in optimal shape should you decide to venture there. Why? Well, heading to Vegas is like taking an express train straight to HELL—but actually enjoying the ride!

In the end you either love it or hate it, but the experience is a MUST for all. Vegas is by far the most draining and treacherous getaway I've ever been on, but it's also the absolute most fun an adult can possibly have (hopefully without losing your house or requiring the aid of a bail bondsman). There's a saying that people actually "age" when they're in Vegas, but damn, it is worth it, because you honestly feel like you've lived SEVERAL lifetimes by the time you pack up your bag and head home.

The energy starts pumping through your veins the second you spot those bright lights while landing. Then you literally hit the ground running (hence the optimal-shape reference) and you are in for an intense full-body workout.

Okay, but why will it drive your husband nuts if you venture to Vegas? The reality is you might actually forget you HAVE a husband while you're there! The mind-blowing array of hotels, clubs, shows, spas, shops, and restaurants alone will make your head spin. It's like a giant cocktail party and you've got VIP access. But you can ease your man's worries by reassuring him you won't be doing anything too risqué (except for that "Stripper 101" class you signed up for, which could actually benefit him in the future). Oh, and he might have some slight reservations about those tickets you booked for the "Thunder from Down Under" all-male revue show, featuring those exquisite hard-bodied blokes from Australia. Celebrity-spotting is always a blast, and since anything can (and does) happen in Vegas, you too could be swept off your feet by the very dashing George Clooney (or any of the original *Ocean's 11* crew!) Since you are going with your closest (and hopefully wildest) gal-pals, the sky's the limit. Speaking of limits, it's best to limit calling home as much as possible, which will just add to your husband's torture and keep his imagination reeling. Be safe, and good luck hitting it big. Vegas is waiting. Start with a shot of tequila and GO!

99 *Assign Him to Day-Long Diaper Duty*

I know I'm not the only mom who has ever wondered how it is that something so offensive can come from such a small, adorable human. Babies are a true wonder in so many ways, but somehow they are born with a temporary internal recycling

RISK INDICATOR: 1
You're in the Clear
Can you help it if Baby Mikey can't stop eating broccoli? If your husband starts whining about his day-long sentence, just say, "Hey, you wanna make it a *week*, Mister?" That should shut him up.

plant that turns everything into bright green watery oatmeal with the distinct aroma of rotting eggs and burnt mushrooms. I admit to dry-heaving on occasion while changing my infant son. I didn't see it coming, though. I honestly believed everything my sweet offspring would do (or expel) would be perfectly tolerable simply because I'm his mother, but what can I say? I was wrong. Unbelievably wrong. There are just some baby bowel movements that should only be handled by hazmat professionals. So if moms can be thrown by an especially dirty diaper, you can imagine how dads feel.

Yup, if your boy (the big one, that is) has been naughty, assigning him diaper duty seems divine. Before announcing his punishment, feed your baby some yummy prunes or fresh peas. Either one will do the trick.

100 *Surprise Him with an Exotic Pet*

Ferrets are actually illegal in some states. I'm not sure why, as they're pretty much harmless. Smelly, yes. But harmful? Never. But they are considered an exotic pet, and by that I mean high-maintenance and ridiculously expensive. They are the kind of pet you wouldn't want to receive as a

RISK INDICATOR: 4
Watch Your Back
I don't know about you, but I don't like the idea of a scorpion running loose in the house. Buyer be warned.

gift, let's say at Christmastime when you thought you were finally going to get that Tiffany diamond necklace you've been dreaming of for years. *Ahem.* The giving of any "pet" as a gift is generally a bad idea because the recipient is suddenly saddled with . . . WORK! For example, when a silly ex-boyfriend of mine decided to give me the gift of a "smelly weasel" (a.k.a. ferret), I was thrilled at first (because they *are* very cute) but then quickly realized I was going to be annoyed and poor for quite some time. I had unfortunately lost my dog, Bandit, that year, but I was in no mood for a replacement pet—especially one that is naturally hyperactive, and needs to be "descented" by a vet to live among humans! Ferrets also come with a long list of do's and don'ts. Example: DO get gouged by purchasing "organic" ferret food, but for heaven's sake DON'T leave the bag out where your ferret can get to it, because it will eat right through it and probably through your furniture if you're not watching. So you get the picture here. If you want to give your pet-loving pookie a pile of headaches, get him an exotic pet to love and care for. Snakes, chinchillas, scorpions, and squirrel monkeys also qualify.

101 Celebrate "Lorena Bobbitt Day"!

As you can see, we saved the best—and most extreme—for last! This should be a national holiday, but since that will never happen, here's what I recommend. Ladies, mark your calendars for June 23rd and head down to the nearest bar for a toast to

> **RISK INDICATOR: 4**
> *Watch Your Back*
> Need I say more?

Lorena! Getting some T-shirts made will definitely add some cheer to the occasion; something like "LORENA IS A CUT ABOVE THE REST" should definitely do. Inviting the husbands is only appropriate, although I wouldn't be surprised if they decline to join the festivities. But between us, you gotta admit Lorena was one screwed-up lady. I've thought of many ways to punish my husband (most of them involving slow poisoning), but actually slicing off his kibbles and bits never occurred to me for a second! First of all, the mere idea of blood freaks me out and I couldn't imagine the carpet-cleaning bill after such an ordeal. Plus, thinking about committing such an act is one thing—doing it is quite another!

But that is precisely why Lorena should be honored, and why it will drive your husband totally bonkers when you pay tribute to this historic (and quite deranged) female figure. Here's my personal toast: "Lorena, wherever you are, we want you to know that even though we don't condone the disfiguring of men, we completely understand how a husband can drive you to the brink of insanity. However sick and twisted your attack was, the idiot you were married to should have known better than to mistreat you (and leave kitchen knives just lying about). Your shocking story will be passed down through the ages—a strong reminder to all men not to screw with the wrong bitch."

Cheers!

Conclusion

My Dear Fellow Torturer,

Just because we've reached the end of our journey doesn't mean the fun is over. Think of all the laughs we've had, and how much we've grown. If anything, this book is a testament to the power of female bonding. We **need** each other to get through those tough times with men (that's why there are more of us and less of them.) Remember, I will always be here for you (as long as you don't kill anybody because I'm not doing jail time). I encourage you to keep this book handy, and crack it open anytime you need to indulge in a good fantasy, but if you want to keep in touch . . . have I got some news for you!

Torture is going viral, baby, so jump online and join the revolution at *www.101WaystoTortureYourHusband.com*. Make it a bookmark, tell your BFFs about it, and let healing begin. Legions of women feel the desire to torture their mates from time to time, and now you know it's completely acceptable. (Oh . . . and one more thing before we're done: if this book ever becomes a movie, à la *Sex and the City*, I really hope to see you there. The drinks will definitely be on me!)

Okay, let's recap before we wrap things up. Remember, ladies:

1. Husbands *can* suck.
2. You are not alone.
3. It's okay to be devilish.
4. Cover your tracks.
5. If busted, deny, deny, deny.

Happy torturing!

About the Author

Maria Garcia-Kalb's book was born of sheer frustration following her surprisingly stable twelve-year marriage to a man she says **still** doesn't know her exact bra size—despite their lengthy union. According to the author, "A man will never remember his wife's measurements, exact birth date, or favorite color, but ask him for Kobe Bryant's stats and he'll regurgitate figures like Dustin Hoffman in *Rain Man*."

When Maria isn't busy dreaming of ways to torture her man, she is a beloved and award-winning radio broadcaster, with more than fifteen years of experience in the exhilarating world of FM radio. The author currently resides in Manhattan with her family.